*Body, Spirit
and Democracy*

Body, Spirit and Democracy

DON HANLON JOHNSON

North Atlantic Books
Somatic Resources
Berkeley, California

Grateful acknowledgement is given for permission to quote from the following works:

Quatrain #2 from *Unseen Rain*, by Rumi, translated by John Moyne and Coleman Barks. By permission of Threshold Books, RD 4, Box 600, Putney, VT 05346.

"At Blackwater Pond," from *Twelve Moons*, by Mary Oliver. Copyright © 1977 by Mary Oliver. First appeared in *Commonweal*. By permission of Little, Brown and Company.

"Some Questions You Might Ask," from *House of Light*, by Mary Oliver. Copyright © 1990 by Mary Oliver. Reprinted by permission of Beacon Press.

ISBN-13: 978-1-55643-166-1

Published by North Atlantic Books, P.O. Box 12327, Berkeley, California 94701 and Somatic Resources, P.O. Box 2067, Berkeley, California 94712

Cover art: *Summer Body* by Roz Driscoll
Cover and book design by Paula Morrison
Typeset by Catherine Campaigne
Printed in the United States of America

Body, Spirit and Democracy is sponsored by the Society for the Study of Native Arts and Sciences, a nonprofit educational corporation whose goals are to develop an educational and crosscultural perspective linking various scientific, social, and artistic fields; to nurture a holistic view of arts, sciences, humanities, and healing; and to publish and distribute literature on the relationship of mind, body, and nature.

Library of Congress Cataloging-in-Publication Data

Johnson, Don, 1934–
    Body, spirit and democracy / Don Hanlon Johnson
       p. cm.
    Includes bibliographical references.
    ISBN 1-155643-166-X
       1. Mind and body. 2. Mind and body therapies. 3. Body, Human—Religious aspects. 4. Body, Human—Social aspects. 5. Body, Human (Philosophy) 6. Johnson, Don, 1934–   . I. Title.
BF161.J593 1994
128—dc20   93-49887

2   3   4   5   6   7   BERRYVILLE 11 10 09 08 07

For my mother, Josephine Hanlon Johnson, whose vitality at eighty-five years of age testifies to the intimate connection between physical health and spiritual commitment, and for Mike, Mora and Rina.

ACKNOWLEDGMENTS

A GROUP OF Somatics innovators has been especially close to my giving shape to this book: Judith Aston, Bonnie Bainbridge and Len Cohen, Emilie Conrad Da'Oud, Robert Hall and Charlotte Selver. Bonnie, Emilie and Charlotte generously shared the details of their life with me and edited the sections of this book which deal with those details. Somatics psychotherapist and my wife Barbara Holifield has read every draft and given me invaluable feedback. Michael Murphy, founder of Esalen and author of The Future of the Body, has nurtured my work for over two decades.

My work of recent years has brought me into contact with a group of people from radically different ethnic backgrounds: first nation people Joseph Couture, Maggie Hodgson and Pamela Colorado; long-time leaders of the freedom movement Vincent and Rosemarie Harding and their younger colleagues Clyde Ford and Kathy Washington; and Leonid and Dmitri Spivak of St. Petersburg. Our growing friendships have given me an unusually intimate sense of the richness of intelligence and healing capacities from which I had been alienated. The generosity of Laurance Rockefeller has made it possible to nurture these relationships around the theme of "The Body and Spirituality." The Fetzer Foundation also made a contribution to this project.

First-hand experience of healing is the most effective teacher of matters related to this book. Since the publication of my last book, *Body*, four healers have played an important role in my life. Dr. Ching-Chun Ou, a Buddhist physician, has with her needles lifted veils of pain which before her work I had assumed were a natural part of my personality; and in the doing, taught me about compassion. Dr. Eliott Blackman, an osteopath of the old manipulative school and a homeopath, enabled me to discover for the first time a sense of liquidity in the formerly arid regions of my spine. Michael

Salveson, a senior teacher and practitioner of Rolfing, helped me recover my original sense of the power of that work in liberating me from pain and narrow-mindedness, a sense that had been obscured for reasons I describe in the book. Justine Fixel, an elder Jungian psychotherapist, guided me through two divorces and two deaths of loved ones, helping me contact unsuspected resources of self-healing and imagination.

Mary Anna Eckberg, an outstanding Somatics clinician and my companion for nearly ten years in shaping our program of graduate studies, has taught me about how to combine gentleness and courage. Ian Grand, Tina Stromsted and Judyth Weaver, who have joined our faculty along the way, constantly enrich my grasp of the nature of our common work.

The California Institute of Integral Studies has been a fertile place for writing this book. President Robert McDermott and Dean Jurgen Kremer have enthusiastically supported my giving time to it. A group of faculty—we call ourselves "The Dawn Seminar," from our early morning meeting time—have read some of this manuscript and given me invaluable feedback: Tanya Wilkinson, Mike Acree, Eva Leveton, Elinor Gadon, Daniel DesLauriers and Judy Schavrien. Our graduate students have consistently helped me clarify my work by their questions, objections and enthusiasm.

My writing friend Sandy Boucher helped me weather the periods of despair that go with this sometimes lonely work and helped me clarify language and concept. Richard Grossinger and Elizabeth Beringer, this book's publishers, have warmly encouraged my work. It was a privilege to have Lindy Hough as an editor because of her intelligence and thoroughness.

Elizabeth Behnke, the founder of The Study Project in the Phenomenology of the Body, read an early version of this manuscript. Her brilliant synthesis of phenomenological analysis and Somatics practices has been a major inspiration for me.

Others who have kept me going by their friendship and by giving me support in other ways have been Basil Anderman, Steve

Donovan, Bokara Legendre, Susan Griffin, Dulce Murphy, Roxanne Lanier and Michael Marsh. Roz Driscoll generously contributed a reproduction of one of her artworks for the cover.

James Ogilvy played a distant yet essential role in the generating of this book by his invitation to join his project "Revisioning Philosophy" which put me in touch with many of the people mentioned above.

TABLE OF CONTENTS

Points of View

The center clears. Knowing comes:
The body is not singular like a corpse,
but singular like a salt grain
still in the side of the mountain.

Rumi[1]

Twists and turns in the route that my life has taken have been mild in comparison to the sharp and tortuous ones that confront a large percentage of human beings. None of my ancestors has ever been torn from home in the middle of the night, deported to a faraway camp, tortured, raped or murdered. I have never been denied entry to any segments of society because of my ethnic background or sexual preferences. I have not been uprooted from my homeland by invading armies, to travel across vast distances, to build a life in a foreign country whose language I did not know. I have never been in prison. Neither the conflicts within my family nor my physical constitution were enough to drive me to the point of suicide, substance addiction or clinical madness. I have only a vague feel for what it is like to have cerebral palsy or multiple sclerosis or for what a paraplegic has to cope with. My challenges include the commonplace ones of depression and boredom, along with a life-time of back pain and the emotional scars of two marriages ending in divorce. And I have had to find my way out of a maze of highly effective brainwashing techniques which left my soul depleted well into middle age.

It has been difficult for me to draw the map of the route I have taken simply as it is, neither overly dramatizing it with apocalyptic colors, nor reticently failing to acknowledge the gods lurking in its modest contours. Only recently have I come to realize that my story is simply mine, that it does not need to be evaluated by comparison with others' stories, nor do others' need to be translated into mine. Not surprising that it took me so long to appreciate that obvious fact: I spent nearly half a century in institutions organized on the basis of stories which were held to be normative for all human beings, stories into which all other stories were to be translated — sometimes by force, more commonly by intellectual and psychological persuasion.

Baptized as an infant into Roman Catholicism, I was taught that I had a knowledge about the true reality of things inaccessible to outsiders. As a young adult, I joined the religious order of Jesuits, the avant-garde of the papal army charged with bringing that truth into the far nooks and crannies of what was thought to be a largely ignorant world. When I left the order fifteen years later to marry, I became a practitioner of a recently founded school of body therapy known as Rolfing. There, to my eventual embarrassment, I found myself once again within a community which believed that truth in its fullness was accessible through a single gate, in this case, through a precisely defined alignment of muscles and bones.

Catholicism, the Jesuits and the Rolf Institute existed within a larger social milieu which was itself the bearer of canonical stories about gender, cultural differences and political authority, in the light of which many other stories were invalidated.

According to the teachings which shaped me, a pluralistic community, in which many stories coexist, was something to be tolerated either as an unavoidable evil or as a step along the way to that utopian moment when the world will embrace one viewpoint.

Precisely because the defining stories preserved in the institutions which I fit myself into are held to express the truth for all human beings, authority is a central issue. When the stakes are as high as eternal salvation, enlightenment, or, at least, the truth of things, one cannot rely on the vagaries of individual judgment or democratic consensus. Someone with assured reliability has to determine which of many stories are accurate and to perpetuate the orthodox stories without contamination. To that end, all of the institutions within which I spent my life developed sophisticated practices for shaping adherents to experience the world precisely as described by their stories. As you will find out in subsequent chapters, that shaping is a very physical activity, involving the patterning of muscles and bones, the habituation of bodily responses and the disciplining of the senses.

I use the word "stories" instead of "belief systems" or "philosophies of life." When, in the manner of an archaeologist going through a dig, you sift through the baroque layers of logic and abstract theories about the world, you eventually come to a very human story about an individual or a community struggling to make sense of the complexities of everyday life. If those unique stories have faded from memory, either because they occurred too far back in history or because the individual would rather forget them, the religious and philosophical ideas distilled from them easily take on the air of eternal truths, valid for all. Reconnecting those abstract theories to the original lived stories is a crucial element in making room for a pluralistic world which not only tolerates but actually relishes many versions of reality.

In the spirit of Twelve Step meetings and native American circles, I tell in this book a number of stories of my journey and those of others. I use the stories to illustrate how the most seemingly abstract notions about life are distilled from experience. By constructing the book in this way, I join many others — activists, intellectuals, artists, religious workers — who are attempting to articulate how we might actually accustom ourselves to embracing a pluralistic world as something more desirable than any of our authoritarian monistic alternatives.

The relentless homogenizing forces presently at work endanger more than species of trees, birds, fish and family grocery stores. Many ancient communities fervently continue their missionary attempts to establish the hegemony of one religious story over all others. Marxist and scientific atheists look for all religious stories to be replaced by mathematical and quantitative descriptions, which some of us would also call myths. Freudians, Jungians and Reichians each attempt to reduce those stories to their particular version of psychodynamic myths. Those few groups who embrace a world of many stories stand out in their rarity: native Americans, some African religions, some sects of Buddhism and Hinduism and marginal groups of intellectuals and artists.

As you will see in subsequent chapters, my path out of a dogmatic monism involved learning the full implications of the obvious but usually taken for granted fact that each of us has a different point of view. I mean that literally. Becoming familiar with my walking, breathing and gestures, along with associated impulses, thoughts and images, dissolved the tenacity of the dogmatic beliefs in which I had been schooled. As I came to feel, not just acknowledge philosophically, the uniqueness of how and where I stand on my uniquely shaped feet, I came to realize that my more abstract ideas about such exalted matters as morality and death bore the idiosyncratic marks of my high-arched feet and hummingbird-like hormonal rhythms. At the same time, I began to feel that other points of view contributed perspectives that I could never reach from the narrow peninsula on which I stand.

Any literal point of view represents the crystallization at a unique moment and place of a wide variety of factors. Some reflect the stances which populations are prompted to take from such primordial forces as religion, biological or social evolution. Others are idiosyncratic, like the peculiar ways the vertebral bones in each of our spinal columns are differently arranged. I know that it is an unfamiliar line of reasoning to argue that we perceive the world differently because I stand or sit in a place that you do not, on feet or buttocks with different shapes than yours, innervated by a somewhat unique nervous and hormonal system, with a different metabolism, shaped by the peculiar events of my history and ideologies. Yet, I believe there is an elaborate web of intimate connections among seemingly ethereal notions about reality, narrow-minded attitudes towards other people and very fleshy postures and emotional reactions.

It is precisely the literalness of points of view that distinguishes a healthy pluralism from widely discredited amoral relativisms which argue that any set of values has equal status with any other. There are some metaphorical points of view which would obliterate the literal. The abusive parent and the political torturer would destroy the other person's standing, moving and speaking. The colonialist would uproot ancient communities from the lands which make sense of their spiritualities and healing practices. Religious, philosophical and therapeutic ideologies would have people believe that the way they stand in their peculiar space is a source of error to be corrected by reliance on officially sanctioned perspectives.

There are some points of view which are more healing than others. For many of us, with our varying histories of infant terrors and childhood obedience-training, it is the task of a lifetime to gain a truly healing point of view. The fear that shapes our flesh in those early years situates us within an enclosed region from which it is difficult to realize that what we see from here is so little of what is. Such a perspective is typically narrow in feeling, often mean-spirited, making it hard for us to appreciate both ourselves and others. A point of view is healing when it gives a panorama spacious enough to make it obvious that my particular location gives access only to a limited region; without information from people situated on those far distant mountains, valleys and coasts, I and those near me are condemned to make sense of life with the merest fragments of truth.

MANY PEOPLE HAVE analyzed how abstract theories veil their origins in individual viewpoints expressed in personal stories. I have chosen to focus on three particular components of any point of view:

1. The region called *body,* which refers to things like muscle tone, excitement, digestion, semen, sensory perception and death.
2. The region traditionally associated with *spirit:* grand things like purpose, love and vision.
3. The kinds of authority to which one turns in moments of crucial decisions about basic human values.

Throughout the book, I use italics for *body* and *spirit* to undercut a widely held misconception. Until recently I had been misled by thinking that those realities are substantial *things* at which one can point. On that assumption, I labored under the illusion that the Roman Catholic Church, the Jesuits and other religious organizations are primarily occupied with spiritual matters; body therapies and medical disciplines, with the body. But I came to realize that *body* and *spirit* do not stand for identifiable objects: they are names which people use to indicate different aspects on the continuum of human experience. In that sense, religions are just as preoccupied about what they call *body* as Somatics therapists are about what they identify as *spirit.*

LIKE ANY NAMES, *body* and *spirit* have a contextual history, both within a given culture and from one culture to another. Differences in definitions are not simply semantic. They reflect radically different norms in light of which people make choices about such crucial matters as healing, sexuality, work, politics and death. I want to sketch a few classical variations on the definition of *body* and *spirit,* and how these particular definitions have been concretized in specific forms of authority.

Plato argued that the true self is in the grip of a *body* conceived of as a wild animal. Its unruly urges required taming by gymnastic, music, the arts, mathematics and philosophy so that the self, liberated from seductive desires and illusory sensations, might ride peacefully into the world of the True and the Good. Platonic thought described spiritual life as a progressive journey away from ephemeral physical realities into the realm of immaterial eternal ideals. In his view, authority belonged to those few who had succeeded in breaking the fleshy chains of feeling and sensing that imprison human beings in the cave of illusion. Conceiving *body* as a wild animal driven by irrational desires and sensations, and *spirit* as the realm of logical, philosophical and intuitive reason eventually infected a less dualistic Aramaic Christianity and laid the groundwork for the Western educational and political institutions within which many of us were shaped.

The Mosaic tradition is one example of a contrasting set of notions. The patriarchs and prophets conceived of human beings as fully embedded in this earthly life. Although Yahweh was absolutely transcendent, religious practice focused on those activities that carried on God's creativity: working the land, serving family and neighbors, caring for the sick and the poor and especially procreating children. There was neither a vocabulary nor a set of practices that separated *body* from *spirit*. The question of immortality was not even raised until very late in Jewish history. In contrast with Platonic elitism, the Mosaic model of authority was more functional. Some men by lineage had a particular knowledge of all the ramifications of the law and the intricacies of ritual. Others demonstrated a particular skill in more complex spiritual problems. Because of the central importance of procreation in the spiritual life of Judaism, mothers had a particular authority. Because religious practices were home- and meal-centered, Jewish women gained a ritual authority that was denied their Christian counterparts.

In Buddhism, there is a common teaching that any distinction between *body* and *spirit* reflects existential conflicts between such

7

things as love and duty, head and heart, man and woman. These are not thought to be essential divisions in reality but problems arising from the peculiar character of human life. They can be transformed from conflicts to paradox by the practice of such psycho-physical disciplines as meditation, sacred dance and the movement arts in which a practitioner typically comes to the experiential realization that such dualisms are mind-made illusions. In contrast to Western mysticism, where the practitioner attempts to extricate him or herself from the sticky world of senses and feeling, Buddhist practices take a person directly into that world by cultivating attention to sensing, breathing and body movements. Authority takes a somewhat confusing form. On the one hand, some Buddhist theory seems to undercut any kind of hierarchy based on distinguishing the essential wisdom possessed by one person from that of any other. That notion, however, seems to have had little effect when viewed against the older and more dominant, hierarchical caste systems of Asia, with their rigid structures of authority, both political and spiritual, and gender differentiation. I will examine such paradoxes in detail.

Early Christianity introduced a radically different twist on the conceptualization of these realities, rife with paradoxes that will unfold in succeeding chapters. The gospel teachings that Jesus was God in the flesh and that he physically rose from the dead and ascended into a physical heaven were interpreted as divinizing the human body and the material universe. That theology, heir to the earlier Jewish tradition, explicitly rejected Gnostic conceptions of the body as separate from the soul. But unlike the predominant teaching among their Jewish forebears, the founders of Christian theology argued that the body was eternal. Our bodily senses and impulses cannot be transcended because they will be with us forever, in the delights of a very sensual heaven or in unrelieved torment in what are believed to be the physical fires of hell. That bizarre set of beliefs (whose strangeness is often concealed under a veneer of banal religiosity and abstract theological language) led Christianity, particularly in its esoteric monastic forms, to develop an elaborate set of technologies to transform bodies from what Saint Paul calls *sarx* ("hunks of meat") into *soma*, the quivering flesh of Christ.

In addition to those older notions, many of us have been deeply affected by a major shift in the conceptualization of *body* and *spirit* and authority which began to take shape in the seventeenth century with the beginnings of modern science in the West. Vesalius, Descartes and Galileo introduced the notion of the body as a dissectable thing, obedient to mechanical laws like any other object. This *body* did not even possess the animal passions of Plato's *body*, let alone the more human qualities of freedom, creativity and compassion: such qualities, according to religiously minded thinkers, belonged to the radically different world of spirit. To secular thinkers, those qualities were only mythical notions used to express what has not yet been reduced to physicalistic causal explanations.

The new empiricism had an enormous impact on the definition of authority, which shifted from religious faith to experience. This paradigmatic shift is commonly thought to be the foundation of modern democracy, a society based not on a privileged knowledge, accessible only to a few, but on public experience, available to all. In fact, "experience" in scientific thought became narrowly defined as sense data purified by instrumental measurement and described mathematically. Those data are no more accessible to ordinary people than are the sacred texts of established religions. True authority, in this model, is restricted to that small cadre of people trained in the methods of modern science, a new priesthood.

The native American view of bodily reality is very different. In stark contrast to the rapacious philosophies of their colonizers, native peoples conceive the human being as spiritually situated with animals and plants within the seasons, nourished by the earth. In contrast to the absolutely transcendent Jewish Elohim, the Christian Holy Trinity and the Plotinian One, all peering down from an infinitely high summit, the many divinities of the native peoples emerge from the earth, bearing the shapes of animals, plants and human visions. Native spiritual practices are of the body: hunts, harvests, races, dances, fasts, sweats and feasts. In

9

contrast to the Western scientific definition of experience, this more ancient tradition looks to bodily experience as the bearer of an order and wisdom all its own, irreducible to the narrow abstractions of measurement and mathematics.

I HAVE GIVEN this brief sketch of culturally diverse ways of thinking about body, spirit and authority as a preliminary taste of how we might loosen up the rigid dogmas which surround those ideas. We are buffeted by unnecessary conflicts in the contemporary world between *spirit* and *body*. The realities signaled by these words are often severely at odds with one another. The price paid for their quarrels is high. Spirituality to the purely scientific or political mind often seems escapist, non-scientific and anti-democratic, a way to avoid the bleakness of a violent and polluted world or to simplify a far too complicated one. *Body,* disemboweled of vision and purpose, is left to the manipulations of technicians and cosmetologists. It wanders aimlessly in the world of hard work, fighting, pain and death. Modern medicine, exercise technologies, even secularized acupuncture and herbalism treat human beings as if inflamed muscles, viral invasions and arterial clotting exist in a realm apart from one's emotions and visions about the meaning of life.

But if you look at the origins of these words, you will find little reason for their tendentious relationships. *Body* derives from an Old High German word, *bottich,* which means brewing vat, the place for distilling spirits from grains and fruits. For several centuries *body* meant the whole person—"what is a body to do?" "If a body meet a body ..." *Spirit* in a wide variety of languages means breath and vitality; it refers to such human qualities as the good-humored twinkle in a friend's eye, a clever story which breaks a rigidly held position, the soft and open face of love. It also refers to the special refinements of the life of a particular human community that derived from seasonal rituals, chanting, postures, visualizations and physical manipulations.

Spiritual teachings are not about the ethereal, but about the nearest-to-hand, stripped to its bare grain of irrelevant gloss, calling people to return to essentials obscured by layers of conventionality. Spirituality, in more ancient connotations, is abstract only in the sense that certain forms of music, painting and writing are abstract. Or that cognac is abstracted from grapes. It is about the immaterial only in the sense that vapors are less dense than the liquids from which they are being distilled.

Spiritual stories and practices are the most refined products of a geographically situated culture. A people makes its characteristic liqueurs—Armagnac, slivovica, vodka, Scotch—by subjecting local grains or fruits to processes of distillation, which have been refined and handed down for centuries. In the same way, a particular cultural group selects from the infinite experiences which constitute its history certain key stories and retells them from generation to generation—the infant Moses being plucked from the rushes, Jesus battling Satan on the West Bank, Gautama sitting by the Ganges. Out of all the possibilities of gesture, posture and movement, it ritualizes a few—those which have associations with crucial events in the life-cycle or with desired states of peace or reverence or which remind the community of important experiences in its history. The group gradually weaves together its stories, songs, dances, architecture, cuisine, art, styles of work and healing practices into the single cloth we call its spirituality. The vocabulary of that tradition will be taken from the recurring cycles of birth and death, the weather, shapes of the terrain, the surrounding animals and vegetation, the physical styles of work, healing and shared visions.

Such classic texts as the Bible, *Koran, Upanishads* and the *Tao Te Ching,* unlike the abstract commentaries written about them, are also experiential. They are the stories of peoples making sense of their journeys through different lands, their healing experiences, how their sages went about their lives. They are cast in the sensual imagery of how streams wear away stones, of sexual intercourse, storms blowing through valleys, the sound of the lute played by a man weeping for his lost country.

Spiritual practices embodying those teachings have always been radically experiential, having to do with birth, sex, work, disease and death. Some of those practices are designed to give people a clear sense of our concrete situation within the earth. For example, the elaborate system of hatha yoga *asanas*, like native American rituals, originated in attempts to gain a sense of unity with the different beings that make up the physical universe: lotuses, scorpions, lions, deer, buffalo, rainstorms, quiet breezes, imaginary demons. Jewish davvening, Christian kneeling and Buddhist bowing manifest physical experiences of awe in the presence of the sacred. Sufi whirling reconnects one with the movements of the stars and planets. T'ai chi chu'an imitates the coiling of serpents engaging herons in combat. Other practices are specifically designed to give the practitioner a sense of the worlds of meaning within one's own skin. They enable one fully to inhabit one's breathing, viscera, running, fear and sexual excitement. They create a sense of a home from which one can journey into the wilderness of exotic states of consciousness and return to the safety of the familiar. A home that can endure the dislocations of war, disease and the death of loved ones.

That radically experiential quality of spirituality accounts for the little-noticed fact that the history of formal religions is a record of periodic breakdowns in a culture and its conceptual systems followed by a return to origins. At such transitional moments, a community is driven to regain a sense of the difference between the basic and the conventionally religious. The Jewish prophets angrily called their people back from empty formalisms to fundamentals of devotion to Yahweh and love for their neighbors. Gautama immersed himself in learning a multiplicity of traditional Vedic practices; when they ceased to have meaning for him, he stopped and found the meaning of truth in quiet sitting. Jesus claimed to teach nothing new, simply a return to the love which had been neglected in the panoply of religious observances. Luther's Reformation, profiting from the results of the first printing of the Bible, called ordinary people to return to the simple biblical stories uncontaminated by the arcane theologies spun out by priestly specialists.

Such crises, which are found again and again in all the major spiritual systems, have counterparts in more primordial traditions. The initiation of shamans among native peoples, for example, deliberately provokes a breakdown of how they see the conventional world. The shaman-to-be is typically subjected to rituals, wilderness journeys and psychotropic plants which obliterate any notion that the vastness of reality can be snared by any set of words or ideas.

A predictable move during any such breakdown, personal or social, is to return to the familiar stories. One sees it now throughout the world in the many movements back to fundamentalist religion. But there are structural problems with simply returning to the old stories as they are.

No doubt, the old stories told in the classic texts express messages about love, truth, compassion and service that easily strike valid and truthful chords in our hearts. But those teachings are often situated in climates, cultural eras and languages that are foreign to our sensibilities. For those of us who grew up in the New World outside of tightly organized clans based on ethnic similarities, the founding stories of Christianity, Judaism, Buddhism and Islam are at several removes from our journeys. They speak of attitudes and mores that are out of place in our complicated, pluralistic society. In hard-to-translate Aramaic, Hebrew, Sanskrit and Arabic, stories tell of wanderers having strange visions in desert worlds, of animals in tropical forests, nomads fighting battles over seemingly trivial stakes, inspired teachers persecuted by functionaries in now extinct political systems. Spiritual teachings can seem ghostly, added on to the world that confronts our senses: that of work and pain, films, personal computers, city design, rap music and cyberaesthetic. Brought from the Old World like family heirlooms, those teachings evoke nostalgia for beautiful things left behind and memories of pains and oppressions better forgotten. The traditional rituals, hymns, sacred architecture and art are like museum pieces created by someone else whose sensibilities are remote from our own.

Within any particular spiritual tradition, the primal stories are

13

derived from journeys through sensually familiar lands and climates, involving groups of people who spoke languages similar to theirs, with familiar songs, dance and adornment. You can get a sense of the contrast to our own situation if you think of places where the original sensual matrix for the spiritual stories is still relatively intact: the Middle Eastern deserts of Islam, the Himalayas of Tibetan Buddhism, the banks of the Ganges, the arid mesas of the Southwestern United States and the highlands of Mexico and Central America. For us relative newcomers to this New World, however, those sensual roots are obscure, creating a deep fracture between our everyday sensory experience and structures of spiritual meaning. The design of our cities, churches, the workplace, schools, the calendar of holidays (previously "holy days") no longer reflect a shared faith.

In addition to that obscurity of the sensual basis for the traditional stories, there are more serious problems with those stories as they stand.

For one, the primal stories, which led to the creation of the major spiritual communities, were created within a hierarchical context in which democratic values were not even a question. Only one person or a few were thought to have the full access to the truth; others were to submit to them. Moreover, the classical stories, and particularly the theological commentaries which mediate those stories to us, are predominantly told by men, often men of a narrow class within society. As such, they leave out the experiences of women, children and men of marginal classes. In fact, the tales of the relations between *body* and *spirit* which will occupy much of this book often take for granted the subjection of women, children and slaves to men who were in positions of power.

Even more seriously, the old stories are rife with images of communities embattled by outsiders who are thought not to possess the Truth. Israel at war with the Canaanites; Christians organizing ghettoes, pogroms and Crusades; Muslims in conflict with Armenian Christians, indigenous African religions and Hindus; Seventh Day Adventist missionaries trying to convert Brazilians and Samoans.

There is nothing radically new about our particular plight. Humanity has seen one pilgrimage after another, in which old cultures are replaced, usually with violence, by others. The displaced refugees must always negotiate a new peace with the cosmos, in a new climate, with new perspectives. So with us, most of whom are no more than two or three generations removed from refugee families. A new culture may be in the making. It is emerging among people who have a shared sense of a single community of human beings sharing a single planet with limited resources. The people in this community are aware of history, have traveled, know that there are many different expressions of basic human values. They read books and watch television. Such people are sceptical about belief systems which exclude people because of gender, color, sexual preference or class.

Our task is the ancient one of looking deeply into our shared experiences, and telling, like recovering addicts, the stories of how we got here, not simply in words, but in gesture, song and image; sharing the ways we have healed ourselves and learned to cultivate states of consciousness which transcend everyday banalities.

I have shaped this book in that spirit. In subsequent chapters, I describe the six elaborate shaping practices or "technologies" that created the skeleton of my own stories. Three of those can be found within identifiable institutions: Roman Catholicism, the Jesuits, and the Rolf Institute. The other three are the more difficult to discern, ubiquitous forces of ethnicity, politics and gender. In each case I will show how body-shaping methods correspond to a particular community's understanding of *body* and *spirit*.

I give particular attention to how the ideas and practices exemplified in those particular technologies have seriously impaired our ability to construct a genuinely collaborative society, in which people of radically diverse points of view can work together towards common goals. Later chapters show from a Somatics perspective how a study of failures within these six areas can yield insights in how to go about shaping a more democratic community.

Somatics

My ability to articulate the themes of this book comes from my twenty-five years of study and work with an unusual band of people in a little understood field that others and I have called "Somatics."[2] Their sensitive touchings and words have made it possible for me, approaching sixty, to enjoy ranges of movement and absence of physical pain that I did not know when I was thirty. And unexpectedly, they helped me recover a sense of spirituality which was fading when I first met them.

In the popular mind, Somatics is "New Age," born at places like Esalen Institute in California during the 1960s and later. The truth is that the field dates back to the Gymnastik movement which was set in motion by a number of teachers who traveled back and forth between Northern Europe and the Eastern seaboard of the United States during the mid- and late-nineteenth century: François Delsarte, Genevieve Stebbins, Bess Mensendieck, Leo Kofler, and Emile Jacques-Dalcroze, to name a few.[3] These people shared a new vision of embodiment that was at odds with the dominant models found in classical ballet, physical education, religion and biomedicine. Instead of training dancers and athletes to shape their bodies to fit a classical form, considered normative for all, they encouraged individual expressiveness and a return to a more "natural" body. Rejecting biomedicine's and religion's separation of the human spirit from a mechanistically conceived body, they envisioned an intimate unity among movement, body structure, health and spiritual consciousness. At a time when medical doctors were still engaged in the most crude uses of surgery and medication, the practitioners of various branches of Gymnastik were already doing sophisticated healing work using expressive movement, sensory awareness, sound, music and touch.

The World Wars loom large in the shaping of this movement. The first war rent the international and interdisciplinary community of dancers, physical therapists, craftspeople, artists and scientists, leaving the schools of body-teaching intact but isolated.

16

The second war dispersed the pioneers, forcing many to put aside the more visionary aspects of their work to eke out a living as refugees by practicing what looked like physical rehabilitation or psychotherapy.

In the 1960s the hospitality of Esalen Institute in California and a counter-culture exploring different states of consciousness provided the opportunity for a regathering of strands of the widely shared vision that had been lost fifty years earlier. A new cooperative venture began to form. Some of the old pioneers traveled westward from New York and Boston, gathered large numbers of students, returned to the Eastern seaboard, established new schools and often eventually brought their work back to Europe where it had been forgotten. By the end of the 1980s, there were international conferences on Somatics in Paris, Zurich, Naples, Montivideo, Montreal, Strasbourg, San Francisco and New York.

Still on the fringes of society, often labeled quacks by conservative physicians and psychologists, these thousands of educators and healers practice such methods as Sensory Awareness, the F. M. Alexander Technique, Gerda Alexander's Eutony, Rolfing, Moshe Feldenkrais's Awareness through Movement and Functional Integration, the extended family of practices based on the work of Wilhelm Reich, the Lomi School, Continuum, Aston-Patterning, Body-Mind Centering, Trager Work, Hakomi Work, Rosen Work, Breyer Work, Process-Oriented Psychology, the movement work of Mary Whitehouse and a host of others.[4]

Although there have been no significant empirical studies of Somatics methods, tens of thousands of people attest to their efficacy.[5] The diversity of our claims indicate how Somatics crosses the boundaries of the established disciplines of psychotherapy, physical therapy and education, medicine and meditation training. For example, widely reported outcomes include successes in addressing:

   • Chronic physical symptoms: back pain, whiplash injuries, various forms of arthritis, scoliosis, the restrictions of cerebral palsy;

- Emotional or psychological complaints: depression, sexual disfunctions, body-image problems, substance addictions, relationship problems;
- Improvement in capacities for focused awareness and stillness required for the practice of meditation;
- Increase in everyday flexibility and vitality.

IF YOU COULD wander about as an invisible observer, you would see the practitioners of these methods sometimes kneading muscles, moving bones, giving movement or awareness suggestions. Some would be touching lightly; others vigorously and deeply, often simply listening. People who come to us are generally referred to as "clients" rather than "patients," to signify the more active role assigned to their participation in the work. Sometimes those clients are clad in underwear and lie on special tables designed for "body-workers," sometimes they are dressed in leotards and are moving around what might be a dance studio, sometimes they are dressed in everyday clothes and sitting in chairs. Some practitioners have the air of craftspeople working with ancient furniture. They approach their clients with an impersonality that is not quite coldness, but more a reflective focus on the minute details of the grains of connective tissue and bony contours. Others exude the personal warmth that typically evokes psychological material. Still others would be more colorful, more in the line of choreographers and performance artists.

Few practitioners enjoy the security that comes from membership in a publicly sanctioned professional field. Those who have licenses to practice have them from another field—medicine, psychology, physical therapy, osteopathy. Most of us have been circumspect outlaws. Some have been subjected to lawsuits for practicing without licenses; a few have been jailed.

But despite the mottled and sometimes contentious differences in method and style among these thousands of workers, we share a vision about the nature of reality which has more in common with older multicultural ideas than with modernist European scientistic notions. That vision has to do with the significance that we assign to the awareness of physical processes in the life of the human spirit. Bioenergeticists, Rolfers and Feldenkrais practitioners argue about many things. But they all make the common assumption that sensing, feeling, breathing, moving, postural changes and sexual excitation are crucial factors in the human search for meaning. Whether one is being prodded by a Rolfer's elbow, vibrating under a Reichian's palm, or trying to concentrate on the sensual effects of the disorienting Feldenkrais movements, he or she is constantly reminded that the realities lumped under *body* or *spirit* are experiential: aching muscles and constipation at one extreme; love and the bliss of cosmic harmony at the other.

This book is about that shared vision, not about the technicalities of Somatics. You will discover a great deal about the actual methods by indirection, just as you get to know a person better in the course of living with him or her than through explicit self-descriptions. The structure of the book reflects the healing process itself, which takes place more by indirection than by direct onslaught on the obvious symptoms. The essential nature of healing shows itself in the relief of chronic stress in response to the unsolicited loving touch of a friend, a rush of joy at the sound of a piece of music, surprise at a new way to move the spine away from pain or remission of a cancer against all medical odds. By the end of this book, I hope that you will have enough of a feel for the broad applicability of the healing strategies of Somatics that they will be of use in your own struggles.

Somatics practitioners, like psychoanalysts, have a lot to say about how to extricate ourselves from the murky social problems that confront us at this our *fin de siècle*.

I have encountered some direct sources of hope in the course of following out my own modest experiments in applications of these notions.

1. During the past twelve years, my work has centered on creating and directing an accredited graduate degree, state-licensed

program which educates people as body-oriented therapists, preparing them to work with the most serious problems of the inner city: drug and alcohol rehabilitation, schizophrenia, hospices for people dying from AIDS, healing survivors of political torture, suicide prevention, and sexual and physical abuse. The program was created in 1978 by Will Schutz at Lone Mountain University under the degree title of "holistic studies." I joined it when it moved to Antioch San Francisco, took over its direction in 1983 and changed the name to Somatics. We have since moved to the California Institute of Integral Studies after a brief stint at New College of California, when Antioch went bankrupt. During those sometimes bleak years, we have witnessed a significant shift in cultural attitudes towards the body. At the outset, both other faculties and directors of clinics considered our work to be "touchy-feely" and narcissistic in nature; our graduates had to be quiet about their unique training in touch and movement, disguising themselves as conventional verbally-oriented psychotherapists. Now, there is growing and widespread recognition of the power of sensitive touch, body movement and breathing work in the most difficult healing processes. Several colleges have imitated our own curricular approach.

2. Prompted by our natural concerns about the widespread politically sanctioned abuse of flesh, a group of us have created a Healing Center for Survivors of Political Torture, funded by the United Nations and other organizations. I have been touched by the generosity and passion with which people of many healing skills from diverse cultures and religious backgrounds have volunteered their services to meet the needs of refugees in the Bay Area.

3. For several years, I have received funding to bring together major innovators in Somatics with Christian, Buddhist, Islamic and Hindu spiritual leaders, along with elders from various native peoples to share different healing traditions and spiritual practice. In our many gatherings, I have found that immersion in touch, breathing, movement, sound and feeling provides a refreshing relief from the verbal debates that too often obstruct the efforts of good-willed people to collaborate.

4. In another project, I have brought together leading biological researchers with Somatics practitioners to investigate the healing efficacy of Somatics practices. In these ongoing research design seminars and in their implementation, I have been struck by the openness of these scientists, reflecting their commitment to alleviating the serious pains of fellow humans. This commitment transcends the medical and economic dogmatisms that too often constrict the healing process.

There are many such projects afoot in the world. Western medical practitioners have become increasingly aware of the efficacy and even, in specific cases, the superiority of indigenous systems of healing. Western physicists are beginning to acknowledge the wisdom in Asian and native American cosmologies, previously thought to be "merely" mythical. Philosophical and literary intellectuals increasingly speak out against the persistent tendency to organize people and their thinking under one logic. This book is offered as a modest contribution to those many efforts to preserve our richly nuanced world with its proliferation of many exotic species and human cultures against the onslaught of both violent and non-violent homogenization.

SECTION I

Body-Spirit Institutions

Is the soul solid, like iron?
Or is it tender and breakable, like
the wings of a moth in the beak of the owl?
Who has it, and who doesn't?
I keep looking around me.
The face of the moose is as sad
as the face of Jesus.
The swan opens her white wings slowly.
In the fall, the black bear carries leaves into the darkness.
One question leads to another.
Does it have a shape? Like an iceberg?
Like the eye of a hummingbird
Does it have one lung, like the snake and the scallop?
Why should I have it, and not the camel?
Come to think of it, what about the maple trees?
What about the blue iris?
What about all the little stones, sitting alone in the moonlight?
What about roses, and lemons, and their shining leaves?
What about the grass?

Mary Oliver, "Some Questions You Might Ask"[6]

2.

Incarnation: Roman Catholicism

I WAS BORN into a web of paradoxes surrounding *body, spirit,* and democracy, confusions woven into the fabric of my family in which my father and mother inhabited conflicting points of view. From my non-religious father, a construction worker, master of the physical world of work and sports, I learned to associate the body with the hard work which we, like Adam, were cursed to do as men, to feel it as a beast of burden eventually to be discarded. He worked in the heat, dust, cold and rain of the Sacramento Valley six, sometimes seven, days a week, building houses, highways, waterways and heavy pipelines, a life which left him bent over in old age from muscular exertion, and with emphysema. On the rare days when he was not working, he hunted, fished, played handball, basketball and poker at the Elks Club and drank with his friends. Grandpa Jul was like that too, a hardworking carpenter who was roofing a grain elevator on the Sacramento River right up until the week he died as an old man. He taught me how to play pinochle and drink beer when I was only four. Both of them exuded the anti-hierarchical spirit of their pre-Christian Scandinavian heritage, a democratic spirit that survives today in Iceland. They railed against religious and political totalitarianism and the pretentiousness of intellectuals.

My father urged me to develop myself physically, building me a hanging bar and basketball net in our backyard, teaching me to bat and catch a ball, and taking me out on his hunting trips. I had trouble with all those activities, feeling clumsy and weak. Told by our family doctor to avoid any exercise that might provoke my chronic asthma and to avoid being out in pollen-filled winds, I was encouraged to spend a lot of time resting in our house with the windows closed. That angered my father who wanted me to take my place at his side in the hurly-burly world of men.

Under the guidance of my Roman Catholic mother, I got a very different sense of the body. She is quiet and unassuming, with an erect posture and a lifelong history of virtually perfect health. She was always sensitive to my needs and nurturing, sometimes to a fault. Her concerns about my health gave me a sense of my body as easily subject to damage and illness, something to be cared for with an attention bordering on obsessiveness.

Her religion, into which I was initiated as an infant, put transcendent stock on that bodily attention. Catechists, nuns and priests schooled me to feel that the body was our unique point of contact with the divine, our immortal companion in the physical fires of hell or the sensuous bliss of heaven, depending on how obedient we were to the laws which governed its most minute acts, even its perceptions.

My mother's submissiveness to an explicit hierarchy of authorities—husband, priest, pastor, bishop, Pope, in that order—was the antithesis of my father's profanely democratic attitude.

Those conflicting views of *body, spirit,* and democracy did not have equal value. Catholicism intruded itself into my sinews with a strength disproportionate to its role in my ancestry. My mother and her Irish-born father, Joe Hanlon, were from the only Catholic branch of my family. His wife and my father's parents were all Protestants, some Lutheran, some Presbyterians. They were cynical both about secular and religious authorities, having at best a condescendingly tolerant attitude towards exotic Catholic rituals, moral strictures and papal imperialism. And yet my mother was formally charged with my spiritual life by virtue of a contract demanded of non-Catholics marrying Catholics that their children be raised Catholic. This arrangement was sure to create troubles, causing me to feel that neither my father nor most of my relatives had the capacity to grasp the important truths about reality which were accessible to me even as a young child. I became a battleground, not only of faith, between my parents, but of attitudes towards the body and sexuality.

I found the physical world of my father repugnant. I didn't like spending summer vacations in the intense heat and dust of the Sacramento Valley, riding around with him and sitting for hours in his pickup, living in hot noisy motels on the outskirts of one-horse towns like Escalon and Manteca, where he had to stay to supervise the construction of heavy pipelines. I was ill at ease being a child around men who were drinking and fighting and bored by sitting with them listening to prizefights and baseball games on the radio. I often got asthmatic seizures when I had to get up at five o'clock on starkly chilling winter mornings to slush through rice paddies and sit with my father in duck blinds. I got restless sitting motionless for hours by a creek, ravaged by mosquitoes, waiting for my father to hook a trout.

In contrast to my father's backbreaking physicality, the spiritual life of my mother and Grandpa Joe, as well as their quiet kindness, were more comfortable and aesthetic, making it an easy option for me, no matter what their contractual arrangements about my religious education had been. Its center was the cavernous Cathedral of the Blessed Sacrament, a block from the California State Capitol. They would take me there early on Sunday mornings while my father was still asleep, where an Irish priest, dressed in gilded silks, quietly reciting Latin in a thick brogue, performed the magic rite of changing bread and wine into the body and blood of Jesus. Barely tall enough to reach the top of the bench where we knelt, I was mesmerized by the enormous marble altar with six golden candelabras, in the center of which was the gem-encrusted, silk-covered home of Jesus, the tabernacle, lit by the deep blues and reds of the stained glass windows depicting magical events from a strange past, with the sounds of an enormous pipe organ bellowing from far up in the choir. I understood very little of all this; I did know that it spoke of a life radically different from that outside in my father's world of physical labor.

✿

I HAVE A chronic back problem. I was only four years old when our family doctor first noticed its symptoms. In the course of examining me for a fever, he asked me to touch my chin to my chest. I couldn't; I never have been able to. Fearing spinal meningitis, he ordered me to the hospital. They found no infection. Radiologists eventually isolated a congenital connective tissue disorder called Forestiere's Syndrome or non-ankylosing spondylitis (an ankylosing one progressively distorts the spinal column). Although my vertebrae and disks retain their integrity, the connective tissue surrounding them calcifies, blocking inter-vertebral movement. I have never experienced the world within a normally mobile spinal column, one that twists, leans sidewards, curves forward and back in the usual way. Living in a professional field that pays great attention to patterns of movement and posture, I am often embarrassed by not being able to do things that others can do, like rotating my torso to look easily at the person next to me.

✿

WITH NO BROTHERS or sisters, I spent hours each day reading. My favorite books were Frank Baum's *Oz* novels. Life around me in the physical world seemed like Dorothy's Kansas—flat, boring, holding out only a promise of growing up to become a hardworking adult restricted by a family, finally to die and probably end up in the eternal fires of Hell or the shorter-lived charcoals of Purgatory. I longed for a cyclone to carry me away from that fortress world into a magic land filled with magicians and faerie queens. Because of asthma, I was often in a drugged, trance-like state brought on by an opiated cough syrup called sedatol and a crude early form of benedryl. After school, while other boys were playing outside, I would lie on my bed for hours in a stupor, tossing in the air one of my seven solid rubber dwarfs, usually Doc, entering Oz. Imagining myself dressed in white silk robes like Erroll Flynn, I would lead bands of thieves into high mountains where we would slay evil occupants of hidden palaces. I would become the new king, borne on bejewelled litters into vast marble throne-rooms where I would sit high above my thousands of courtiers. At five o'clock I would turn on my Philco radio and listen to Captains Midnight and Silver, and Superman, slowly returning to Kansas in time for dinner with the help of more ordinary men like Jack Armstrong and Tom Mix. I got to spend hours in Oz on Saturday mornings, turning on the radio at ten o'clock for "Let's Pretend," followed by the Metropolitan Opera, lasting late into the afternoon.

This physically passive, yet actively wild fantasy pattern of my daily life was not a matter of a brief period of childhood: it lasted throughout grade school and high school.

My mother not only introduced me to the fantastical world of religion, but also to another region that I would come to associate with *spirit:* the music, literature and history for which others in my hardworking family had neither time nor taste. She bought me my first classical records when I was in first grade: the toreador aria from "Carmen" and Schubert's "Unfinished Symphony." I lay on my back for hours listening to those records, imagining stories to fit the music. I much preferred that supine world to the raucous boys' world where I got bronchial spasms and always dropped the ball.

Had you asked me in those days what *spirit* meant, I would have located it in the colorful world of my fantasies, classical music and novels, as well as the ritual world of the Cathedral, apart from the ordinary. The physical world was where I wheezed, had hives and got beaten up by other kids who called me a momma's boy because I didn't develop my muscles and I was clumsy at softball and basketball. It's where I got tired and sick: the world of *body.*

Spirit was that magic land populated by the Blessed Virgin Mary, the Infant Jesus of Prague, my guardian angel, Satan, Saint Francis, Caliph Haroun el Raschid of *1001 Nights* and Alexander the Great. One got there by being swept away by other-worldly forces like drugs or prayer.

☙

I AM CONSTANTLY STRUCK by a wide gap between my experience as a child and adolescent in the Church and the popular notion that Roman Catholicism is ethereal, unrelated to the body. I found the exact opposite: concern for the body was everywhere. As early as third grade when I was being prepared for First Holy Communion, a Franciscan nun taught us the basic driving idea behind that obsession, one that I would hear again and again in more sophisticated, theologically elaborated forms in high school, university and theology school: the central belief of Christianity is that Jesus rose from the dead, claiming an immortal body, our promise of immortality. Saint Paul says that Christianity stands or falls on the truth of that belief. "The trumpet will sound and the dead will be raised incorruptible, and we shall be changed. This corruptible body must be clothed with incorruptibility, this mortal body with immortality" (1 *Cor.* 15.52). The meaning of the Resurrection, I learned in those early years, is that God and the physical cosmos are united in the body, fundamentally in the body of the risen Jesus; by extension in the bodies of those of us in whom Jesus lives through baptism. The sheep will be sorted out from the goats at the Last Judgment by this standard: the saved are those who recognized the divine in the hungry, the poor, the imprisoned, the thirsters for justice; the greedy and envious are left to burn in their flesh. God, said Athanasius, is no longer invisible.[7]

Infamous Catholic guilt is rooted in that teaching. Because the body is believed to be the home of the divine, its behavior in the most minute details is of eternal significance. What constitutes the proper kinds of bodily conduct is the subject of endless scrutiny by Church authorities. It is unthinkable that puzzles about sexual intercourse, masturbation, homosexuality, birth control or abortion could be left to the vagaries of personal judgment, let alone to the immature judgment of a young boy. Any mistake in these matters might have eternal consequences.

At early morning catechism classes, held on Saturdays for public school children like myself, I was introduced to the inner essence of Catholic life which Sister Felicia described as the progressive transformation of mortal and sin-prone flesh, *sarx*, into the sensitive, immortal and luminescent *soma*, the body of Christ. That change would be effected by the sacraments, for which we young boys and girls were being prepared; they are the key to understanding how *body* and *spirit* function in Roman Catholicism.

"Sacrament" means a tangible, visible reality which serves to manifest the invisible divine. (Ida Rolf, the creator of a Somatics method which I describe later, repeatedly used that term to describe the significance of bodily structure, visible tensions in the neck, for example, manifesting invisible spiritual and psychological tensions.)

Once Jesus departed this planet for what we were told was a very bodily heaven somewhere else, the loss of his physical presence was made up for by the seven sacraments of the Church: the immersion of the naked infant into water, the confirming slap on the cheek of the adolescent, the laying of hands by the bishop on the priest being ordained, the rubbing of oil on the sick person's five senses, the accurate description of sins into the priest's ear, and the eating of bread and drinking of wine consecrated during mass. (Conspicuously absent from that list is the sacrament of marriage about which little of specificity was taught in our early catechism classes. Only in high school would we learn that this sacrament cannot be completed by words of the ceremony alone. The actual insertion of the husband's condom-free penis into his wife's diaphragm-free vagina is an essential element of the ritual. Without it, the marriage is not considered valid and can be annulled if evidence can actually be marshalled to prove lack of "consummation"—

31

the reason for the public showing of the bloodied wedding-night sheets as part of Mediterranean wedding ceremonies.)

I was taught that devout attention to the physical details of the sacramental rituals was the fundamental way whereby we could directly contact the divine. It was precisely the physicality of these practices that distinguished us Catholics both from my Protestant relatives and from our Japanese Buddhist neighbors who, we were told, considered that material reality was only a way-station, shortly to be left behind.

The theology of the Eucharist, which we were about to receive, is one of the most dramatic examples of the extreme physicality of Roman Catholic belief. Some of the many theological disputes over its literalness have ended in physical violence and officially mandated executions. I was taught that the wafer I swallowed at Communion was literally the flesh of Jesus. At the consecration during mass, the bread lost the nature or "substance" of bread to become a new substance, the body of Jesus, hidden to unbelieving eyes by the deceptive sensory manifestations of bread. "Transubstantiation," it was called in our catechism—a change in the very essence of a physical reality without a change in its sensible form. And by extension, we who ate that flesh were being changed in our very bodies into the immortal flesh of Christ.

Protestants, Sister Felicia explained to us, argued that the bread and wine only "stood for" the body of Jesus, the Eucharist having no spiritually transforming qualities apart from the uprightness of the communicant. Such a view, according to our faith, incorrectly substituted language and mental attitudes for physical practices, removing God to a realm that was outside the palpable cosmos.

While we were being taught to believe that our rituals were putting us into immediate contact with the omnipotent creator spirit, our bodily behavior was carefully regulated to mask the exotic nature of the belief. To receive Holy Communion, you would think that we, like human flesh-eaters in other cultures, would manifest our belief in the outlandish nature of that act with painted bodies, wearing loin-cloths, drumming, chanting, dancing ecstatically.

Instead, we dressed in white shirts and ties, processed demurely up the nave, eyes cast down, hands folded in front of the chest, singing in thin voices:

> O Lord, I am not worthy
> That thou should'st come to me
> But say the words of comfort
> My spirit healed shall be.

Kneeling at the communion rail, we modestly opened our mouths, stuck out our tongues to receive a paper-thin white wafer, returned to our pews and knelt in silence. An uninformed outsider would have no idea that we were convinced that we were eating the flesh and drinking the blood of an embodied God who had triumphed over death.

That disparity between rigid bodily expression and wild spiritual belief set up a conflict in me that would take me decades to unravel. It was an embodiment of a Manichean theology of eternally divided dark and light, two warring parts of me, one absolutely good, the other a companion of the Prince of Darkness, irredeemable. The core of the dualistic teaching comes from the ambivalence of the official church towards the nature of inner experience. In those early catechism classes, the sister and the parish priest taught that my body—its movements, impulses, sensations—was sacred, the medium of my contact with the divine. But at the very same time, they said that those impulses were not mine: their final ownership depended on the final outcome of the cosmic battle between God and Satan, each struggling on the battleground of inwardly felt fantasies and physical desires to gain the upper hand. It was a terrifying picture. Like any child, I was beset by night terrors, strange demons and powerful bodily sensations. I frequently walked in my sleep, and woke the house with my screams. I remember falling asleep fearing that I might awake in hell. In that atmosphere, it made perfect sense to develop a constant vigilance in the fear that letting down my guard for a moment would be enough for a demon to trap me.

"You must put on the armor of God," St. Paul exhorts, "if you are to resist on the evil day; do all that your duty requires, and hold your ground. Stand fast, with the truth buckled around your waist, and integrity for a breastplate, wearing for shoes the eagerness to spread the gospel of peace and always carrying the shield of faith so that you can use it to put out the burning arrows of the evil one. Take the helmet of salvation and the sword of the spirit...." (*Eph.* 6.11–17).

Although that battle was painful, its drama was more captivating to my youthful imagination than the dull haze of everyday valley life. And even my chronic illnesses and physical weakness had no bearing on success or failure in the internal coliseum where Jesus and Satan waged their eternal contests.

In seventh grade, I left public school for Saint Francis Catholic School and had an opportunity to connect my inner life of fantasy with the outer world of elaborate ritual by becoming an altar boy.

When one entered the sanctuary to perform the sacred liturgy, every element became an expression of the divine. Until the late 1960s, when many of the old forms were dissolved by the Second Vatican Council, every movement and gesture of the priest was carefully prescribed. When reading the orations and passages from the Four Gospels, for example, the priest was to open his hands and arms in the archetypal manner of prayer and the people were to stand; when reading passages from the Old Testament or from the Epistles, he was to rest his hands on the missal while the people sat; after turning the bread and wine into Christ's body and blood, he was to keep his thumbs and index fingers joined until the end of mass when the altar boy had washed his hands. The altar in every church had a small stone in its center containing bones of martyrs. At defined moments during the mass, the priest kissed this stone while his assistants bowed. Ritual bows were made to the crucifix above the altar and occasional genuflections, most on one knee, some on two. There was a definite way for the priest to turn from the altar to face the congregation, always clock-wise, as in native American circles. At solemn masses, the pre-scriptions were even more elaborate. For such occasions, the priest was assisted by a deacon and a subdeacon, also ordained officials. Since they participated in the omnipresent hierarchical form of the Church, there were different qualities of bows and different numbers of waves of the bronze incensers accorded to each. While the priest-celebrant received a deep bow from the waist and three swings of the censer, the deacon received only a bow from the shoulders and one swing. By the time the altar-boy reached the lowly congregation with his censer, he gave a slight nod with the forehead and a peremptory swing to each section of the church.

Saint Francis, of all the churches in Sacramento, prided itself on its elaborate choreographies. There were precise places for each type of server to kneel, prescribed ways for coming together and turning or crisscrossing to opposite sides of the altar. If you received the honor—by having gained enough seniority—of holding the missal for the reading of the gospel at solemn high mass, there was a special way of supporting it against your forehead. Different depths of bowing were defined: at the *Confiteor* and the *Domine non sum Dignus,* you were to bow deeply at the waist; when the priest approached to have you wash his hands, you bowed only with the head. Washing the hands was one of the more carefully prepared rituals since it could easily have been vulgarized. The priest in his silk brocades and linens sashayed elegantly to the far right side of the altar platform. One server held a cut-crystal (for the bishop, gold) basin. As the priest held his fingers over the dish, the server poured a few drops over them from a cruet. A second server stood holding outstretched between his hands a small linen towel that the priest whisked gracefully away, wiping his fingers as he read the Twenty-Sixth psalm, "I will wash my hands among the innocent. . . . "

There were special movements reserved for once a year. On Christmas Eve at the words of the Nicene Creed, *"Et Verbum caro factum est,"* everyone on the altar fell onto two knees instead of the customary one. At the opening of the Good Friday service, the priests would prostrate themselves for a few silent minutes on the floor of the sanctuary. The most spectacular ritual of the year occurred as the priest intoned the *"Gloria in excelsis Deo"* at the Easter Vigil mass. At that moment, the purple veils which had covered all the statues of the saints and the crucifixes during the forty days of Lent suddenly disappeared, drawn away in a flash by old Brother Ludger's pulling a network of drawstrings that covered the entire perimeter of the church. Some of us altar boys would have the enviable task of shaking braces of bells designed just for this moment. Others would bring on to the altar vases of Easter lilies. The choir's orchestra would belt out chords on violins, trumpets and kettledrums. You knew that Christ was rising from the tomb bringing with him the souls of all the Old Testament saints who had been waiting for him for centuries to lead them, rejoined with their now luminous immortal bodies, into the Promised Land.

When things went well and we all did our part as defined, I had a rare sense of the exact rightness of things and how I belonged, no longer lonely. The hierarchy of the forty men and boys on the altar was signaled by position, gesture and costume. All the groups moved in concert, processing, crisscrossing, genuflecting, bowing at exactly the right moment. I could sense that this chain of being kept on going up beyond the sanctuary through the various levels of saints and angels to the very throne of God. In this divine theater, the carefully choreographed movement was both the very manifestation of God and the means whereby we could experience the life of God. In those moments, the chasm between *body* and *spirit* disappeared. All the material elements of the ritual— bread and wine, costumes, music, moving bodies, resonant voices, incense and the stone church itself—became the body of God.

BUT IT WAS a very male body. There was no question then or now about women being priests. Women were not even allowed into the sanctuary during these rituals, not even to perform the lowest functions executed by young boys. Even now, despite American pastors' widespread refusal to accede to Rome's orders, women and girls are expressly forbidden any formal role in the liturgy, such as reading the sacred scriptures or serving mass. And it was only a small group of men who chose to enter the sanctuary, those with proclivities for lace, incense and theatrical gesture. The viewpoint which I describe here is that of an insider who got to participate in the esoteric rituals. Most men, like women, remain on the far side of the altar rail, unaware of the experiences accessible to those in the sanctuary.

PUBERTY INTRODUCED ANOTHER dimension into my struggles with *body* and *spirit*. Before then, the internal drama between God and Satan ranging in the theater of my inner fantasies and impulses seemed somewhat distant from me. It was indeed inside my skin, but I did not feel that it touched *me*. But sexual desire was a different matter. *I* was aroused; *I* did things about it. On the currents of those new, very physical impulses, the devil seemed capable of riding into the very center of my soul.

My first experiences were with a gang of boys in the neighborhood. We would gather in a secret garage and have orgies of masturbating while looking at bare-breasted native women in *The National Geographic* or nude tracings we had made of clothed women in comic books. When I went to confession, I would say as dispassionately as I could that I had sinned against the Sixth Commandment. "How many times?" the priest would probe. "Oh, two or three," I would mumble, knowing that it was more like fifteen or twenty. "And with yourself or another?" Terrified of being judged a homosexual, which was far worse than a lonely masturbator, I would always say, "By myself." The hitch was that for confession to work, the penitent had to specify the exact number and circumstances of what were called mortal sins. If one willingly lied, the confession was invalid and the sinfulness was even doubled by the sin of lying to the priest. That meant that by the time I had graduated from high school, I had amassed such a debt of group and private masturbations, perverted confessions and criminal holy communions that I could never pay it off except by a Chapter 11 reorganization of my spiritual life.

The genitals are the devil's favorite playground, as well as the bower where one can achieve the greatest intimacy with the divine lover. This dual possibility accounts for two-thousand years of Catholic texts debating how to handle them.

Saint Paul encouraged people to be eunuchs for the sake of Christ. Origen, the great third-century theologian, castrated himself in a fit of Christian idealism. Until this century, it was castrati who had the privilege of singing in the papal choir. Pope John Paul II to this day tells members of Roman Catholic religious orders that their celibate way of life is better than marriage and praises their decision to become "eunuchs for the sake of the kingdom of heaven."[8]

From the earliest centuries, Christian moral texts have given rich details about every imaginable penile sin and its appropriate penance. In a typical passage, the Irish Penitentials, dating back to the fourth century, state: "He who sins with a beast shall do penance for a year; if by himself, for three 40-day periods; if he has clerical rank, a year; a boy of fifteen years, forty days. He who defiles his mother shall do penance for three years with perpetual exile."[9]

Sexual arousal even when asleep troubled moralists. "He who intentionally becomes polluted ("pollution" is the Catholic term for ejaculation; "self-abuse," for the movements leading to it) in sleep shall get up and sing seven psalms and live on bread and water for that day; but if he does not do this he shall sing 30 psalms. But if he desired to sin in sleep but could not, 15 psalms; if, however, he sinned but was not polluted, 24; if he was unintentionally polluted, 15."[10]

The authors of a modern handbook of moral theology pride themselves on finally having arrived at a non-sexist definition of pollution as "complete sexual satisfaction obtained by some form of self-stimulation." They boast: "By evading reference to 'semination' our definition evades the various controversies concerning the specific difference of this sin in men, women, eunuchs, and those who have not reached the age of puberty, since only men are capable of secreting semen in the proper sense of the word."[11]

It is alright for a man, say the moral theologians, "to wash, go swimming, riding, etc. even though one foresees that due to one's particular excitability in this regard, pollution will follow. Similarly, it is lawful to seek relief from itching in the sex organs, provided the irritation is not the result of superfluous semen or ardent passion. In case one doubts about the cause of the itching he may relieve it. It is likewise lawful in case of slight itching if only slight sexual stimulation is experienced therefrom."[12]

To buttress tenuous theological arguments, religious teachers gave us texts written by physicians on the horrors of frequent ejaculation. I read that masturbation is a physical drain dangerous to health: "excessive indulgence frequently causes general debility, weakness, and lameness of the back, dyspepsia, impotency, and predisposition to almost innumerable diseases, by rendering the system susceptible to the action of other causes of disease."[13] Masturbation was said to cause a man's genitals to "shrink and become withered, and cases have been known, in which, faded and entirely decayed, the little remains of them disappeared into the abdomen," making him unable to "penetrate the finest woman in the world." In the masturbator, "[a]ll the intellectual faculties are weakened. The man becomes a coward; sighs and weeps like a hysterical woman. He loses all decision and dignity of character." Masturbators "drivel away their existence on the outskirts of society:... they are at once a dead weight, a sluggish, inert mass in the paths of this busy, blustering life, having neither the will nor the capacity to take a part in the general matters of life."[14]

Catholic control of every act of sexuality is hardly news to anyone. What is not so widely recognized is that sacramental theology represses sensual experience precisely because it exaggerates its importance. Luther and Calvin recognized the exaggeration, arguing that Roman incarnational theology was a form of idolatry, reducing an utterly transcendent deity to tangible, earthly objects, accessible by human activities. They recognized the historical fact that the cultivation of physical states to provoke the furthest reaches of mystical experience laid the groundwork for the Roman hierarchy, within which any notion of a democratic society of peers is unimaginable. In their enlightened yet flawed attempts at a democratic alternative to Roman authoritarianism, they disembodied spirituality, eviscerating the sacraments by relegating them to the realm of imaginary realities. They reduced sexuality to matters of avoiding disease and preserving monogamy.

I was taught that Protestants had spirited the divine to its remote pre-Jesus world beyond the pale of human sensibility. The magic of ritual and ecstatic sexual bliss were banished, leaving only the workaday world of my father and Grandpa Jul.

WHEN THE BODY-ORIENTED practices of the human potential movement became popular in the 1960s it was no accident that there were a disproportionate number of priests and nuns going to places like Esalen Institute in Big Sur, much to the dismay of the secular-minded creators of the movement like Fritz Perls, Abraham Maslow, Carl Rogers and Rollo May. Nor is it surprising that Pope John Paul would condemn the body-oriented meditation practices that are becoming increasingly popular in Catholic retreat houses and seminaries throughout the world.

For my part, by the time I had reached late adolescence in the mid-1950s, seemingly contradictory notions of *body* and *spirit* had rendered me in a state of total confusion about how to shape my life. There was that sick and weak part of myself, often debilitated by asthma. I was small and unmuscular. I felt unattractive. I didn't like sports and physical work. But I had to take my place as a man in the world of work. *Body* was the vehicle for that.

At the same time, my fantasy life continued to flourish, populated now both by lascivious women and heroic ascetics. This was also a very bodily world, filled with rushes of deep excitement, pangs of guilt, very physical longings for something I knew not what. I had been initiated into body technologies that accustomed me to pay close attention to my inner states of feeling and impulse. I was convinced that if for a brief moment I deliberately touched my penis for the sake of enjoyment, or even took a moment's pleasure in looking at my naked body, I might burn for all eternity. On the other hand, I also believed in the sacramental dimensions of that sensitive touch and gaze. After all, it was in that naked body that I was being drawn into the immortal body of Christ. I set out to redirect the urges pulling me into endless sexual fantasies and masturbation towards the mystically erotic world of *spirit*.

A fragment from a passage on heaven from our high school catechism always remained with me. It said something like this: there is little we can really know about heaven. About as close as we come to appreciating its delights is in the experience of orgasm during intercourse between a husband and wife. By then, I was keen enough about ecclesiastical codes to know that the point of that sentence was not about marriage, which seemed a dull affair, and which was, in fact, unfavorably compared to priestly celibacy, but about the experience of intercourse no matter between whom.

The puzzles generated by these conflicts pushed me into a life-long process of inquiry into the nature of sensory experience, touch, eroticism and spirituality.

3

Esoteric Impulses: The Jesuits

IN THOSE EARLY YEARS, I came to be much more at home with the altered states of drug-induced reveries and church rituals than with the ordinary experiences of boys at play and study. The magical quality of those states kindled a passion in me to find a way of living more by their light than by the goals of the everyday adult life of Sacramento. I first got a glimpse of how I might do that when I encountered members of the Society of Jesus, the Jesuits, among whom I would be plunged into an extreme form of body mysticism.

I was a student at their University of Santa Clara. The first person in our extended family to be able to go to college, I chose to go there at the prompting of my father to study engineering as a preparation to join him in his heavy construction business. In my mind, college had nothing to do with Oz; it was a means for moving socially and financially upward as a working adult. I had a hard time with the engineering curriculum, not being engaged by subjects like mechanical drawing, metal shop, concrete stress labs and fluid dynamics. But I stoically accepted it as part of my task of becoming a man and gaining mastery over the everyday. What gripped me were a handful of courses in theology and scholastic philosophy which we were required to take as students in a Catholic university subject to Roman rule. Instead of devoting the necessary time to writing lab reports documenting tests of soil strengths and

43

water pressures, I sat late into the night conversing about the meaning of life with Jesuits who were living as counselors in our dorms. I was intrigued by their life of arcane practices, which went on in secret within the cloister; detached by vow from money and sex, they made no bones about their fervent desires to change the world.

The climax of those four years was a brief two-day silent retreat, which we were required to do before graduating. Those forty-eight hours of silence gave me a sense of peace that I had known before only in brief moments by myself in the woods or sitting quietly in the dark empty neighborhood church.

Upon graduating as a mechanical engineer, I took a job working for Westinghouse in a management training program in Pittsburgh. My life seemed increasingly bleak as the emerald cities of altered states induced by church rituals and asthmatic drugs gave way to analyzing production plans, studying thermonuclear reactors and having two-martini lunches with sales representatives who talked about lubricating oils and packing cases. None of this held my attention. My fellow workers had none of the passion I had seen in my Jesuit teachers. In my few romances, I was constantly on guard, suspicious that every woman might, like Circe and Eve, lure me into a home- and work-centered life that would keep me from ever finding my way along the yellow brick road to the magic world I had only glimpsed as an altar boy at Saint Francis Church.

On Thanksgiving of 1956 I was attending mass at the Pittsburgh Cathedral. While the priest was giving his sermon, I was unexpectedly beset by the notion of becoming a Jesuit priest. Several images came to me in that moment: dressing up in silk brocades and chanting ancient texts like we did at Saint Francis; traveling to exotic places in the world and converting masses of people to Jesus by my inspired preaching; indulging in the study of literature and philosophy. The religious vows of poverty, chastity and obedience suddenly seemed to be the key for liberating me from what I perceived as the deadening path of marriage and ordinary work. Most of all, that life held out the possibility of cultivating the altered states of experience which Jesuits did in the privacy of their cloister. When I let myself entertain that fantasy, I was flooded again with the same sense of peace that I had found during the silence of our graduation retreat. It would stay with me for several years.

The following August, on the festival of the Assumption cele-brating the moment when Jesus raised his mother's body from the grave and swept her away into a very physical heaven, I entered the Jesuit novitiate in the Santa Cruz mountains above San Jose.

❧

My MASTER OF NOVICES was the elderly and austere Father James Healy, infamous among California Jesuits for his obsession with the role of the human body in mystical practices. His daily spiritual talks were collages of passages from books about body reading, phrenology, psychosomatic medicine and hypnosis. He saw these studies as invaluable adjuncts to ancient mystical techniques designed to transform our sarcal bodies into the *soma* of Christ who had overcome the laws of gross matter. He spurred us on with accounts of bodily transformation in the lives of the saints: levita-tion, lack of corruption after death, teleportation, elongation, the frequently reported transformations of body odor into perfumed fra-grances. He kept us abreast of stories about the latest phenomena in the lives of Padre Pio, the teleporting Italian monk, and Theresa Neumann, the stigmatized Austrian mystic whose only food was the Eucharist. If we gave ourselves over to daily meditation, the taking of the Eucharist, fasts and physical penances, we too, he argued, would eventually enjoy such bodily delights.

In his meditation teachings, Father Healy introduced me to rudimentary versions of the more sophisticated techniques which I would later encounter in the Somatic methods of Charlotte Selver's Sensory Awakening and Emilie Conrad Da'Oud's Con-tinuum. For example, using a method developed by Ignatius called "The Application of the Senses," we learned how to reconstruct the sensual details of the events of Christ's life: the lines and textures

45

in his and Mary's faces, the sounds of his voice, the colors and feel of his garments, the qualities of his body movements, the smells of Palestinian dust and sweat, the feel of the heat. In ways that presaged my later work with Wilhelm Reich's orgonomic methods and with Bonnie Bainbridge Cohen's Body-Mind Centering, I learned to pay close attention to different layers of subtle interior movements, said by Jesuit spiritual authors to be clues to the promptings of the Holy Spirit.

I also learned a set of spiritual practices that profoundly disrupted my ordinary state of detached consciousness. It was summarized in Ignatius's Latin phrase *age quod agis* (do what you are doing) meaning that in contrast to making spiritual practice something other than day-to-day activities, it was to be embedded in ordinary life itself. It was a practice which made Ignatius subject to constant harassment from other religious orders for being too secular, for having jettisoned the long periods of private meditation within secure cloisters apart from ordinary life. The practice required disciplining our attention away from internal chatter and fantasy fully into the experience of the activities in which we were engaged, cleaning the communal toilets, serving food, picking grapes, hiking in the Santa Cruz mountains, reading Greek philosophy. Nearly a decade later I would encounter similar practices in Somatics where the emphasis is on cultivating attention to the details of one's physical movements and perceptions. It also characterizes the spiritual orientation of native Americans and Buddhists whose practices focus on the here and now.

Ignatius was famous for having developed a method for steering one's way through the complexities surrounding the making of a major life decision, which Rome correctly perceived as bearing the seeds of anti-authoritarianism. He often was called upon by the secular and spiritual elite of Europe to guide them through such processes, eventually leading to the political influence of Jesuits. He outlined his methods in his little book, *The Spiritual Exercises:* "Three Times When A Correct And Good Choice Of A Way of Life May Be Made," "Two Ways of Making A Choice Of A Way

Of Life In The Third Time," and "Methods For The Discernment Of Spirits, I and II." The techniques teach a person to cultivate non-ordinary states of experience by spending several days
engaged in silent meditation, fasting and physical penances. With
the help of his spiritual director, he is to monitor the various
impulses that come and go throughout the day and night as he
imagines various life decisions—accepting the crown of Hungary,
joining the Benedictine monastery, or going off to slaughter the
Saracens. Each impulse is to be carefully observed as to its qualities
and source: was it accompanied by an erection that led one to fan-
tasize immoral acts? Did it come predictably after eating a bowl
of warm beef stew? in the presence of the crucifix? or did it seem to
come upon one unexpectedly "out of nowhere"?

The "out of nowhere" movement of the Holy Spirit, denuded of
visual or emotional content, prompting an immediate and indu-
bitable response, was the first and superior way of making a good
choice. The entire technology of the *The Spiritual Exercises* was
aimed at evoking that experience. In his early career, Ignatius was
imprisoned by the Spanish Inquisition for that teaching, which
was accurately perceived as anti-authoritarian because Roman
authorities and the sacred texts were in a clearly defined "somewhere." As late as 1989, Pope John Paul II issued a letter con-
demning teachings of a similar sort.

The second way of making a decision was based more on what
we would now call the weighing of feelings and intuitions associated with considerations of the various possible choices, somewhat like the process that typically occurs in modern psychotherapy.
Ignatius called those experiences "consolations" and "desolations."
Although he ranked this method slightly inferior to the first, he
considered it solidly reputable and having the advantage of being
more easily evoked.

The third method, a last resort, was the path of everyday consciousness, the rational approach commonly associated with decision-making: adding up the pros and cons for each possibility in
light of the injunctions of the Gospels and the commands of the

Pope and religious advisers. Although one could live a moral life by obeying one's superiors, secular or religious, or by rational decisions made in the context of long periods of meditation, such an approach was considered spiritually immature, inferior to decisions made solely in light of the personally felt impulses of the Holy Spirit.

Ignatius developed this set of practices for decision-making into a discipline for a radically new kind of monk whose spiritual life would be shaped, not by the physical walls of a monastery and a daily order of community prayer and work, but by a practiced familiarity with, and control over his interior impulses.

Pre-Ignatian monasticism was rigidly contained within the physical boundaries of monasteries under close supervision of religious superiors. That medieval structure evolved out of the painful experiences of the first Christian mystics. Fleeing the fleshpots of Rome for the North African deserts to explore the turbulent underworld of mystical experience, they descended into psychotic confusion living by themselves. Many-headed monsters assaulted them at night in their caves. Exotic women appeared, awakening lusts powerful enough to drive people like Saint Anthony running into Alexandria into the arms of prostitutes. Others, in their mystical identification with the divine, became fanatical cult leaders. By the second century, elder spiritual teachers who had managed to survive the madness of their desert initiations became convinced that it was necessary to take measures for containing the wildness of mystical states. They constructed the first Christian spiritual communities where mystical voyagers could live alone but physically near each other under the guidance of a spiritual teacher who would contest the validity of one's spiritually awakened passions. Men like Pachomius, Benedict, and Bernard of Clairvaux developed a network of spiritual fortresses where mystical excesses would neither sweep away the individual into sin, nor interfere with the outside world, especially with ecclesiastical authority. Individuals outside that system, like Francis of Assisi and Catherine of Siena, were always an irritation to the official church.

Ignatius took on the challenge of creating psychic rather than literal boundaries for an order of mystics who would live in the ordinary world, outside monastery walls, often far away from spiritual authorities. That plan came from a series of visions he received while he was recovering from a cannonball wound he got as a middle-aged soldier during a war among the Basques in the 1530s. The central vision was of a cosmic battlefield on which the armies of Satan were amassed against the armies of Jesus. His divine mission in that war was to create what we might call today a spiritual Special Forces of the Pope, a group of guerrillas trained to go anywhere in the world at a moment's notice to engage in whatever kind of spiritual battle needed to be fought to ensure Christ's victory. In the absence of the external constraints of monastery walls and contact with spiritual authorities, Jesuits had to learn extreme internal controls. They had to become so familiar with their inner impulses, that they would be adept at distinguishing the movements of the Holy Spirit from those of Satan without the help of a near-to-hand authority. In addition, Jesuits had to learn how to domesticate their wide-ranging perceptions and sensual impulses to spontaneously be able to intuit the response of Church authorities in any particular situation. Jesuits were to develop the capacity to renounce their natural tendencies to follow their own perceptions, going so far, Ignatius writes in a famous passage, to agree that what one sees as black is white if one's superior says so.[15]

This passage, written by Ignatius in his *Constitutions*, was the major theme of our novitiate training:

> We ought to be firmly convinced that everyone of those who live under obedience ought to allow himself to be carried and directed by Divine Providence through the agency of the superior as if he were a lifeless body which allows itself to be carried to any place and to be treated in any manner desired, or as if he were an old man's staff which serves in any place and in any manner whatsoever in which the holder wishes to use it.[16]

Ignatius originally wrote this passage for his group of ribald young disciples often living and traveling alone throughout Europe while cultivating intense mystical states. But we were indoctrinated with this image caged within large, carefully controlled institutional settings. Moreover, my congenital spinal disorder had already shaped me to be like an old man's staff. Instead of challenging my growth towards rigidity and pain, this doctrine of obedience actually encouraged it; I was frequently praised for what was said to be my religious bearing.

Ignatius's theology of obedience was a radical departure from previous notions. For his predecessors, it was commendable if the monk or nun simply obeyed the superior even if he or she intellectually disagreed or perceived things differently. But that was not enough for Ignatius. Lacking the safety of monastery walls and easy consultation with a nearby superior, his men had to learn how to *feel* and *sense* what that superior felt and sensed. That extreme version of religious obedience created a pure form of what systems theorist Gregory Bateson identified as the double bind, consisting of two sets of injunctions which seem contradictory:

1. We were to be like a staff or a corpse, passive in the hands of our superiors, knowing that because our various perceptions and impulses could be movements of Satan or God, we had to subject them to the infallible judgments of God's representatives, our superiors. Like the good soldiers who were our models, we were to shape ourselves to embody the will of our commander in the field.

2. But at the same time, the Jesuit was to shape his life according to the inner promptings of the Holy Spirit, not by conformity to exterior commands. The conformist sensibilities produced by military training would never be up to confronting the Brahmins, Mandarins, nuclear physicists, sociobiologists, psychedelic chemists and Sufis with whom Jesuits were routinely expected to truck, working as they do on the frontlines of the Church's incursions into the un-Christian world. Therefore, the Jesuit is enjoined to construct a rococo inner cathedral of fantasies and philosophical ideas, into which he can lure the most clever enemies of the Church and easily

defeat them. Such a rich inner life was bound to inspire deviations from our superiors' commands. The "Rules for the Discernment of Spirits" were prescriptions for radical individuality, if not outright rebelliousness, a characteristic of many Jesuits to the present day.

The paradoxical quality of the rules is not enough to create conflict, for paradoxes are an essential part of becoming an adult; they can even lead to enlightenment if one can discern the rules not as contradictory but as expressions of different ways of looking at experience. For example, those two Ignatian injunctions might be recast in the light of a temporal process of learning. There is an obvious sense in which we cannot trust our feelings, confused as they are by years of enmeshments in family and society; they need to be purged of self-deception in dialogue with friends and teachers who will be honest with us. But there is an ultimate sense in which our feelings are the final arbiter of truth; in Christian theological language, they are where we are touched by the Holy Spirit; in more secular language, our shared and refined experiences are the basis for personal integrity, sanity and democratic decision-making.

The problem lies in learning to discriminate between the layers of self-deception and reliability. Here is where Bateson locates the element that transforms paradoxical rules into what feels like a prison of conflicts: the commands are given without any such discrimination. Moreover, the subject (the child in its mother's arms, myself as Jesuit or later as Rolfer) is not educated to make the necessary discriminations, and is even discouraged from doing so under threat of dismissal from the system (the family, the Jesuits, the Rolf Institute). Here is how Bateson puts it:

> ...the individual is involved in an intense relationship in which he feels it is vitally important that he discriminate accurately what message is being communicated so that he may respond appropriately.
>
> ...the individual is unable to comment on the messages being expressed to correct his discrimination of what order of message to respond to.[17]

In our Jesuit training, as well as in the case of any other human communities ranging from families to corporations, the double bind is not simply an intellectual conflict: it is embodied in gesture, breathing patterns and physical structure. Ignatius had developed a wide range of powerful technologies of the body to transform a group of testosterone-driven young men into a fighting unit that was to be, in the ideal, simultaneously passionately intelligent and totally subservient.

Learning to disengage our bodies from sensual attachments to people and the world was what Ignatius called "the first principle and foundation" of our spiritual practice."[18] His "Rules of Modesty" were designed to shape us according to that guiding image of the old man's staff. We were to walk calmly and erectly, never giving the appearance of rushing. In general, we were to keep our eyes cast down, especially when walking in the streets where we might see a seductive woman or when speaking with a superior to whom we were to embody humility. We were never to speak loudly. Our hands were to be kept at our sides, never crossed in that dangerous area over our laps, nor inserted into our pockets. We were instructed to maintain erect postures in meditation, rigidly kneeling, standing, and in a straight-backed chair or prostrating on the bare floor.

There was more than a casual emphasis on those postural directives. For example, there was the case of the "minor Arsenius." A long tradition in monasticism enjoined monks not to cross their legs, a fault called an "Arsenius" after a hapless monk who, crossing his legs one day alone in his cell, became possessed by the devil, died and went to hell, buried by his fellow monks on a dung heap. Father Healy went one step further, saying that he felt that it was spiritually dangerous for us to cross our ankles, an action called in the spiritual literature a "minor Arsenius." But always wanting to be sure that he was in line with the divine plan, he wrote to the Jesuit General asking if his fears of the minor Arsenius were well-grounded. In the midst of his duties directing a world-wide network of schools, churches and missions, the General thought the matter important enough to respond with a lengthy letter explaining why he judged this to be a spiritually safe indulgence.

❀

WHEN I WAS studying with Ida Rolf years later, I began to understand more clearly the significance of the debate about issues relating to one's carriage. Like Father Healy, she would scold us for crossing our legs; in her classes, we were encouraged to sit primly like Victorians, knees close together, torsos bolt upright, preferably in straight-backed chairs. Her reasoning came from an ancient idea, common to many spiritual traditions, that views the upright human form as the passage between earth and heaven. Verticality is an operative principle in the movement practices of Taoism, Sufism, Buddhism and native American religion. But those older traditions cultivated a vertical torso situated on crossed legs, as in the Hindu lotus posture. Christians considered such practices wise but deficient, embodying what was said to be a passive sedentary mysticism that characterized Asian detachment from worldly activities like helping the poor. In a similar fashion, Ida Rolf argued that the Arsenius, and even more, cross-legged sitting, distorted the relation between the fibula and tibia, which in turn disrupted the overall verticality of one's structure, which was crucial to the development of evolved states of consciousness. And, like Father Healy, she was even a little wary of possible spiritual dangers inherent in ankle-crossing. To their way of thinking, the moment's relief gained by crossing legs or ankles was had at the high cost of stumbling behind in the trek towards absolute truth, identified with a literal vertical alignment of the spinal column.

Here we have moved far beyond the exoteric seven sacraments in which major perceivable events—birth, marriage, death—are thought to manifest invisible spiritual meanings. In these esoteric traditions, the slightest postural change and the most subtle bodily impulse have implications for the spiritual journey. And pre-

53

cisely because of the sacramental character of postural directives, the lines of authority have to be clearly drawn:

1. The alignment of feet, legs, hips, torso and head is an essential means for attaining spiritual consciousness.

2. The definition of that alignment—the precise place for the head to be, for example—is left neither to individual nor communal experimentation, but to external authority. In the case of the Jesuits, it was to be determined by the Jesuit General who was believed to have a mystical connection with God through the Pope. In the case of the Rolf model, the definition of the precise alignment of tibia and fibula was to be defined by what was believed to be her privileged vision of the ideal body structure.

TECHNIQUES OF SELF-TORTURE and public humiliations supplemented Ignatius's "Rules of Modesty." Contrary to popular opinion, these bondage-discipline practices were not aimed primarily at repressing sensual impulses, but on achieving an erotically tinged identification with Jesus who sweated blood in Gethsemane, was whipped, crowned with thorns, spat upon and who carried through the streets of Jerusalem a weighty cross to which he was finally nailed. In that sense, Catholic asceticism is closer in spirit to ritualistic sadomasochistic practices than to colorless puritan austerity, a connection that has often inspired pornographers, like the author of *The Story of "O."*

Catholic churches are filled with sensual images of Jesus dying on the cross, or being tortured at the pillar in front of Pilate, writhing in ecstatic pain, looking not unlike Bruce Weber's scarred model for Calvin Klein's briefs. Medieval art sometimes displays the suffering Jesus about to die crowned with thorns, bleeding from Pilate's whips, with a large erection, a sacrament hinting of the resurrection to come.[19] Nowhere is the contrast between Christian and Indian attitudes towards the relationship between sexuality and spirituality more evident than in the difference between the erotic images of the Jesus invariably linked with torture and the erotic images of men and women in Hindu and Buddhist art, always linked in pleasure.

Father Healy taught us to cultivate what I would now call a homoerotic relation with the imagined naked body of Jesus hanging from the cross, imagining ourselves being embraced, even kissed by him. He gave me a reproduction of a crucifixion by Utrillo, with a voluptuously writhing muscular Jesus, naked save for a wisp of a cloth across his penis. I was instructed to contemplate that image and become one with it. I would spend hours absorbing myself in that image, imagining the pain of the nails in my hands and feet, the pricks of the thorns in my head, the muscular strains in my body. I felt deliciously aroused.

The lives of the saints are typically filled with descriptions of mystical experiences in which pain and sexual ecstasy are linked. Men and women, having inflicted on themselves severe physical tortures, speak of being swept into erotic embraces with the naked body of Jesus, who often opens his skin to receive a man or woman into his spear-pierced breast, or offers golden straws for the saint to suck from his wounded heart.

Following these ancient Christian customs, we periodically beat ourselves with whips and wore spiked chains. Two or three times a week, when the "Flagellation" sign was posted, we would return to our cubicles after night prayers, strip off our soutanes and drop our pants and underwear. At the first bell, Brother Beadle would turn out the lights with a master switch and we would begin whipping our naked buttocks. At the second bell the lights would go on, we would put away our whips and retire. (In later years, I would learn that only California Jesuits whipped their bare buttocks; others kept their pants on and whipped their shoulders.) On certain evenings a sign saying *"Catenulae"* (chains) would go up, meaning that in the morning on rising, we were to wind a spiked chain around one thigh, and another around the upper arm, wearing them during meditation, mass and breakfast.

I reported to Father Healy that I sometimes got an erection

while I was beating myself in the dark and when I felt the spikes digging into my upper thigh. After a few moments of looking out the window at the steep slopes of the Novitiate vineyards with an empty stare, he replied that Rodrigo, brother of St. Teresa of Avila and a missionary who died fighting natives in Brazil, wrote to her of a similar problem.

These torture practices were supplemented by a host of dominance-submission rituals, such as kissing the shoes of fellow Jesuits at dinner, kneeling in the middle of the dining room with outstretched arms proclaiming one's peccadilloes, or eating dinner at the "little table," a regular dining table for eight in the corner of the refectory whose chairs had been removed so that the diners could kneel while they ate.

Because we were practicing techniques designed to produce an eroticism for Jesus, we had to be even more careful that our arousals did not spill over into the devil's control. The transcendental significance of touch was even more emphasized than in my pre-Jesuit religious education. We had a rule not to touch one another, not even in jest, but only when courtesy or playing sports demanded it. There were constant warnings from spiritual directors that to touch one of our brothers would easily lead to "particular friendships," entailing a redirection of our sensual feelings from Jesus to mere humans. For several years, the only physical contact I had with anyone consisted of peremptory handshakes with my parents on the rare visits they were allowed to have with me, and the hug of peace that we were ordered to give to each other during Mass after the 1962 reforms of the Vatican Council. That very absence of touch, with all of the strictures against it and the imagined effects it might have, had of course the effect of stimulating my fantasies about what might happen if I actually did touch someone.[20]

As you might imagine, I became ever more confused about the many desires and perceptions I experienced. I was supposed to cultivate that inner world of feeling and sensation where I would meet my divine lover and learn what he wanted from me while he plied me with the sensual delights that are described in every classic journal of mystical experience. At the same time, I was to treat that world with profound suspicion, aware that the devil might easily disguise himself as the divine seducer. Only those authorities in a direct lineage with God through the Pope could help me from falling prey to such deceits.

Michel Foucault is one of the few secular scholars to have understood that the primary aim of these body technologies was not the repressive one of keeping us from committing gross immoralities; one who was found prone to such immorality would be promptly dismissed from Jesuit initiation. The elaborate strategies were meant rather to develop a complex inner sensitivity to the workings of the divine and the diabolical. The monastic discipline of the penis, argues Foucault, involves a sophistication that rivals psychoanalysis in the subtleties of its discernments of the various states of consciousness. Our practices were directed at creating a gulf between our willful behavior *(spirit)* and the natural impulses of the penis *(body)*, which happened spontaneously and in sleep and dreams. That discipline "has nothing to do with the internalization of a whole list of forbidden things, merely substituting the prohibition of the intention for that of the act itself. It is rather the opening up of an area ... which is that of thought, operating erratically and spontaneously, with its images, memories and perceptions, with movements and impressions transmitted from the body to the mind and the mind to the body. This has nothing to do with a code of permitted or forbidden actions, but is a whole technique for analysing and diagnosing thought, its origins, its qualities, its dangers, its potential for temptation and all the dark forces that can lurk behind the mask it may assume. Given the objective of expelling for good everything impure or conducive to impurity, this can only be achieved by eternal vigilance, a suspiciousness directed every moment against one's every thought, an endless self-questioning to flush out any secret fornication lurking in the inmost recesses of the mind."[21]

Here is the point where theological beliefs about *body* and *spirit* militate against democratic decision-making. The turbulent interior is said to be dark and tortuous; seductions, assaults and the weight of despair can surprise the voyager at any moment. Enmeshed in such deception, one can hardly negotiate the many tricky currents simply on one's own. Safe transit is assured only by absolute dependence on divinely sanctioned guides to whom the wanderer must bare his or her most secret thoughts.

In this point, esoteric Christianity differs from many other spiritual traditions in its notions of sin, hell and damnation. It is easy to miss this profound source of Catholic authoritarianism, confusing it with external political power or psychological manipulation. In the majority of systems of spiritual practice—Buddhism, Taoism, Sufism, Shamanism—the price of not staying to the course of transformation or making errors about how to go about it, is, at worst, being reborn until one gets it right. But in Christianity, one who gets it wrong may burn forever in one's personal flesh. With suffering of that order at stake, democracy is out of the question. As I discovered in years of trying to extricate myself from its tentacles, Roman Catholic ecclesiastical authority is braided into the religiously trained person's very sinews. It gains its hold through shaping people to feel that their inner experiences— images, sensations, feelings, ideas—do not truly belong to them but to the winner of the cosmic battle between God and Satan whose outcome is not known until the final moment of each person's death.

This embodiment of the double bind sometimes felt like it would cripple me. On the one hand, I practiced techniques designed to cultivate and refine my body where the movements of the Holy Spirit were said to be located. My secret world of impulse and imagery was wilder than ever. I was so occupied by legends of hierarchies of spiritual beings and saints, inner philosophical musings about ultimate reality and images of my spiritual destiny, that I could barely see what was going on around me. I had strong feelings about where those impulses were leading me, and they began to lead far from where my superiors wanted me to be. The peace that I had tasted in the Pittsburgh Cathedral was gone.

Out of that fear, I continued rigidifying my muscles, and deadening my perceptions so that I could become *sensually,* not just attitudinally, obedient to my superior. Fervently committed to the ideals of Ignatius, I exaggerated my congenital spinal rigidity to embody his image of the old man's staff more perfectly, to the point where I could hardly bend forward or rotate my head on my neck. I also became his lifeless body. Up until the day I entered the Jesuits, I had intense sexual impulses even though I never dared to have intercourse. Within a few weeks of engaging in Ignatius's spiritual practices, I stopped having those impulses outside of meditation and penances, and didn't experience any until ten years later when I first smoked marijuana. By the time I was thirty years old I was in constant pain, having to get up in the middle of every night to sit until the spasms in my back subsided.

That double bind produced in me a sense of two incompatible worlds: the inner volcanic world of impulse, fantasy and ideas was what I identified as the realm of *spirit.* I viewed the outer protective shell of tense muscles and stiff spine as my *body.*

4

Desires: Primal and Acquired

I GOT THE first glimpses of how to extricate myself from the double bind during the summer of 1960 when I had the opportunity for private study while my fellow classmates were off at Gonzaga University taking courses I had already completed before entering the Order. I was engaged in a stage of initiation which Jesuits call the Philosophate, a three-year study of philosophy at Mount Saint Michael's, a cavernous, neo-Gothic building on a mesa overlooking the railroad yards outside of Spokane. The peculiar energy of philosophy—its passionate inquiry and relentless unearthing of assumed truths—captured my spirit and still does. Reading Plato, Aristotle, Plotinus, Kant and Hegel inspired me to seek the truth just as much as studying the lives of the saints. Their kind of questioning was the way, I sensed, towards freedom and feeling connections with other people.

During this particular summer, left to my own without any formal assignments, I set about reading the complete works of Thomas Aquinas in his original Latin, trying to unravel perplexities about bodily impulses. It was as if I had embarked upon a Western version of *jnana* yoga, a discipline by which the seeker plunges wholeheartedly into intricate systems of abstract thought to the point where the thoughts fall away in exhaustion and the yogi is left face to face with the real.

The confusions I had encountered since catechism about whether or not to follow my impulses, and which ones if any, were formalized in Catholic ethical philosophy. Claiming the authority of Aristotle's *Nichomachaean Ethics,* my high school and college texts said that the good man based his judgments on "right reason." (For forty years until he died, every student at the University of Santa Clara was required to take an ethics course from Father Austin Fagothey whose well-known book was entitled *Right Reason.*) When Aristotle asked himself which of many possible reasons for any course of action was right, he gave the strange reply, "the reason of the prudent man," the man of "right reason." (Women were never at issue in these texts.) His reasoning was that ethical judgments are so complex that there cannot be a logical system for determining the goodness of any particular one. It takes a person who has become practiced in wisdom and goodness to make "right" decisions.

Christian theologians were comfortable with that argument because it justified their demands that Catholics subject their perceptions and impulses to Church authorities—particularly the Pope—who were said to be embodiments of right reason. It didn't take much of a critical faculty to pick out the fallacy in that argument: ecclesiastical authorities, even popes, had often been shown to be erroneous, even morally corrupt. How then could one judge the rightness of their commands if they contradicted one's own sense of what is good and bad? From the time I first studied ethics at Santa Clara, I was troubled by the speciousness of Aristotle's argument. It seemed to vitiate the Catholic claim that its moral philosophy was intellectually respectable. And I was now in my final stages of preparing to teach it.

In my dark and cool basement cubicle, I painstakingly worked my way through worn leather-bound folios of Aquinas with an eye towards sorting out that odd circular argument. Deep into little-read works of Aquinas like the *Summa Contra Gentiles* and the *Commentary on the Ethics of Aristotle,* I stumbled upon lines of reason that had never made their way into Catholic textbooks. To my surprise, neither he, nor his mentor Albert the Great, nor Aristotle himself were the rationalists that popular Catholic teaching made them out to be, but thorough-going experientialists. In passage after passage, I found Aquinas turning to a specific region of human experience as the bedrock both for making ethical choices and for making some sense about ideas of the divine. Specifically, he looked to an area of human experience that manifests itself in two ways: the contemplative spirit of wonder, that radical experience of openness to reality, perhaps most evident in the well-nurtured child; and the primal yearning that is never satisfied by finite achievements. Learning to pay more careful attention to these experiences, one finds a more spacious viewpoint than the everyday, where we commonly feel things like awe, transcendence, what some have called "peak experiences."

Aquinas's baroque reasoning gave me a first clue about how to transform the double bind into a paradox about the nature of experience and set me on the path of investigating the spiritual significance of bodily practices.

For centuries there had been a lively debate among mystics about whether it was possible to have direct contact between a limited human being and an infinite divine. While many argued that they had attained direct experiences of the infinite God and that the Gospels sanctioned such experiences, others argued that such claims amounted to the highest sin of pride, the presumption that finite humans could attain the infinity that belonged to God alone. Aquinas argued that there is a region where human beings have access to the infinite, not in the prideful sense of claiming the divine prerogatives, but in the humble sense of feeling the unbounded yearnings for love and truth. That region can be located only by engaging in practices—meditational, psychological, Somatics—which help shift one's attention from the fear-laden chatter of everyday life towards our primal roots in love and knowing.

Aquinas described a self in which different layers of immediate experiences revealed different qualities. The image of layering enabled him to resolve the ethical dilemma that had puzzled me.

His argument went this way: there are two essentially different levels of human desires, natural and acquired. Acquired desires are the most obvious ones, with no more normative value than the fact that I prefer abstruse philosophy while you turn to poetry instead, or that I choose to live in temperate San Francisco while you prefer the extremes of Manhattan. Another group are the destructive passions of murderous rage, mean-spirited lust and greed. According to the medieval logic of Aquinas—and to the controversial contemporary logic of Wilhelm Reich and Herbert Marcuse—these are not primal, but simply more tenacious and passionate than superficial tastes. Both layers of desire, according to Aquinas, are derived not from the nature of being human, but from a distortion of the process of growing up. Saint Thomas interprets the so-called prudent man of Aristotle, the man of "right reason," as the one who has learned to distinguish between ephemeral "socialized" desires, the deeper neurotic drives, and more basic tendencies, which exist in the region where the human heart longs for beauty, truth, unity and goodness. They seemed to be what Ignatius had identified in "Rules for the Discernment of Spirits" as the motivations experienced "out of nowhere," a simple and direct sense of purpose, the privileged moment of decision-making, the kind of feeling I had in the Pittsburgh Cathedral and at other rare moments in my life.

You, who have not had to disentangle yourself from the elaborate conceptual systems that ensnared me, probably instinctively know that in the most profound questions of life—illness, death, love, birth—the best teachers are not those with bright ideas, but men and women who have gained some wisdom by reflecting deeply on their life experience and who act out of compassion instead of narcissism. I have had to find my way to instinctual knowing by way of such complicated rational manipulations as these.

Thomas's reasoning implied that an ethical life required learning to differentiate between impulses we have internalized for the sake of survival in our particular culture, impressed on us by family and social neuroses, and more fundamental human tendencies.

Contrary to the teachings of popular textbooks and sermons of the time, one was ethical not by virtue of following a rational code of rules but by acting in accord with one's most deeply felt desires. The double bind was transformed into a process of learning through paradox: our experiences often lead us astray, not because bodily sensations are inherently deceptive, but because they require refinement, trial and error, and constant feedback from other perceivers.[22]

❀

AQUINAS'S EXPERIENTIAL archaeology was a foretaste of what I would later encounter among teachers of Somatics who have developed methods for journeying into what Wilhelm Reich calls the biological core of the person. One example is the work of F. Matthias Alexander, who created a method known as the Alexander Technique. In 1887, when he was a professional vaudevillian in Melbourne, Australia, Alexander began to lose his voice each time he went onstage. He noticed that although he could talk through the evening with his friends in the pub without feeling the least discomfort, as soon as he began to take a step towards the stage, he contracted laryngitis. For several months, he spent hours each day recreating his movements in front of mirrors and observing what happened throughout his body. He eventually came to discover an overall pattern of stress which had two components: (1) a postural one which involved the needless tightening of networks of muscles, and (2) a thought component of repetitive ideas about performing in front of an audience, which identified the network of stress as "right." That pattern, which he called "the habit of performance," stood in contrast to his more natural body carriage and behavior while simply conversing in a pub with friends.

Alexander took what he learned from healing himself into work with other people. He eventually came to a distinction similar to the one that Aquinas made between natural and acquired desires. Shaped by years of faulty, even abusive teachings about what he

65

calls "the use of the self," the adult is not in a situation where he or she can trust judgments and decisions based on unclarified feelings. Everyday sensations of how to sit without back pain, how to keep one's eye on a golf ball, how to form words without stuttering, even how to make love, are distorted by learned usage within a skewed social world. To perform such activities properly requires a subtle learning process whereby one learns, with the help of a skilled guide, to reconnect with more trustworthy feelings lodged deep in the organism. Only after a period of such reeducation can one begin to trust one's feelings.

His method, which evolved from those experiments, is now practiced by hundreds of teachers throughout the world. They use a combination of carefully chosen words designed to provoke new senses of the movement—"Let the neck widen," or "Let the waist fall back"—and a very light touch to suggest new ways of moving and to help their clients discover their "habits of performance," the predictable gestural and postural movements which each of us employs in response to situations of stress or discomfort. In that discovery, one typically senses the distinction between the learned stereotype, involving a network of needlessly tightened muscles and a deeper organic self that is more supple, imaginative and innovative.

Alexander's view of how to negotiate the transition from a state where one's feelings are indecipherable and unreliable to a state of self-reliance bear a striking similarity to the mystical tradition. Alexander's key concept was "inhibition," by which he meant not negative repression, but a quiet stopping of one's mechanical behavior, which is addictively directed at some distant goal—sitting in a chair, making money, staying in love. In the manner of meditation, the Alexander student learns to cultivate "non-doing," a sitting with what is, instead of rushing towards that goal. In those gaps, a deeper, more primal sense of movement is allowed to arise. Addiction gives way to conscious choice.

The cultivation of non-doing, designed to interrupt the ongoing rush of mechanical behavior so that a deeper layer of experience

66

might shine forth, is common to many forms of Somatics. The Sensory Awareness work of Charlotte Selver awakens the interest of people in their immediate experience of what they are doing, deflecting it from its everyday obsessions with inner conversations, images or ideas about what is to be achieved. The methods developed by Moshe Feldenkrais, actually inspired by Alexander, use extremely complex movement instructions and manipulations to disrupt the familiar patterns of doing things, so that more organic ways of learning can take place. The work of Emilie Conrad Da'Oud teaches a person to stay with long periods of silence, waiting until unfamiliar bodily movements have time to emerge into awareness. Bonnie Bainbridge Cohen uses her hands to evoke in people an experience of esoteric regions like the *dura mater* of the spinal column with the result that one finds oneself moving at a new and wiser depth of self.

Both my work with Saint Thomas and my later work with the Somatics pioneers signaled a radical shift in my orientation towards the value of immediate experience, both mine and others'. Until this period in my life, I had been barraged by a series of notions that were grounded on the incontrovertible fact that human beings are usually driven by prejudice and often fanaticism, rarely by shared inquiry and the common good. Those teachings were successful in causing me to shrink in terror from any thought of turning towards primal sensual experiences. At the personal level, such a turn was said to put one in danger of diabolic possession: best keep to the clearly defined rules of the Church and the Jesuits, interpreted in specific detail by my religious superiors. At the larger political level, I had been raised on social theorists like Saint Augustine and Thomas Hobbes who argued that strong centralized authority is necessary to ensure order in a community of human beings whose desires are essentially unruly and whose perceptions are fundamentally flawed.

Aquinas's esoteric lines of reasoning gave me hints of an alternative to my fear-dominated state. I got an intuition that I might use all the meditation practices in which I had been schooled, later to be supplemented by psychological and Somatic practices, to sort through the various layers of my experience. For it was true that I sensed deep within me moments of love and compassion and a deep joy. But those moments were submerged in obsessions with everyday concerns and encrusted with profound fear. I also sensed that my outbursts of anger and my frequent descents into depression did not feel like the final story. Would it be possible, I began to ask myself, to allow those fleeting moments of generosity, joy and compassion more space in my life, more authority in guiding me on my way?

I also began to wonder about a different kind of social organization in which people might be educated to sort through the various layers of experience to get a feel for more communal and equitable desires, buried under the fear-induced layers of selfishness nurtured by abstract ideologies. As I was to discover in my subsequent theological studies, several Christian thinkers, including Aquinas himself, had carried that theory of the deep wisdom buried in each human being into a social theory that was a precursor of modern democratic theory. As early as the theologian Marcion in the second century, and continuing through Joachim of Flora, John of Paris and Marcilius Ficino in the Middle Ages, this argument was used to justify a number of revolutionary movements: if the Holy Spirit is poured into the hearts of all people, then the ultimate source of wisdom ultimately rests in those people as one political body, not in a single monarch supposedly appointed by divine right, nor in the Pope himself. The value of any particular form of authority, whether secular or sacred, is proportional to the extent to which it is connected to the wisdom disseminated throughout the social body.

Those two questions—the one about personal transformation, the other about democratic structures—felt like one, for it was the blending of the social order and personal shaping that produced the fearful and brainwashed adult that I had become. Unraveling the results of that shaping had to be both personal and social. From then until now, my work has been characterized by attempting to create social structures—schools, clinics, methods of scientific research—that do justice to primal experiential wisdom scattered among all people.

My first publication was an article about those discoveries, a complicated text with hundreds of Latin footnotes, whose impersonal ecclesiastical Latinized English belies the passion with which I wrote it. It is not the voice of a boy raised in the Sacramento Delta among working-class people, immigrants from Europe, Latin America, Africa and China, none with more than a high school education. My voice was as divorced from the primal realities about which I was writing as were the polite hand-folding and mouth-opening associated with receiving Holy Communion from the primitive ecstasy of eating the flesh of God.

5

Altered States

PHILOSOPHY, DESPITE ITS emotional impact in making me aware
of how brittle my viewpoint had become, was not enough to change
the Saint Paul-inspired character structure that I had developed,
with its fibrous breastplates and spiritual shin guards. It was easy
enough to indulge in a liberated life of the mind while to all eyes I
was physically conforming to social and religious rules. Mind-
altering drugs began to corrode the armor, within a short few hours
blowing open the gates that had succeeded in keeping the flood-
waters of my fantasies and intellectual criticisms safely hidden away.

Before psychedelics caught the public's eye in the mid-1960s,
many Jesuits had joined with other intellectuals in experiments
with the potential of these drugs to enhance meditation practices.
I first heard of LSD in 1963 from an older Jesuit political scientist and theologian, John Courteney Murray. He was a hero for
many of us younger Jesuits, having been condemned by Pope Pius
XII for having written a series of scholarly articles in a theological
journal in 1950 arguing that a democratic society was a better environment for the truly adult practice of religion than a monarchy or
a totalitarian regime. In 1963, when he was in his late sixties, he
had been publicly rehabilitated at the opening of the second Vatican Council by Pope John XXIII who embraced Murray's spiritual
affirmation of democratic institutions.

In between sessions of that Council, Murray had come to the Jesuit house in Los Angeles where I was living to take LSD in an experiment sponsored by The Fund for the Republic, a think-tank under the direction of Robert Hutchins, founder of the Great Books Program at the University of Chicago. He stayed in his room with a tape recorder for three days and left without saying a word to anyone. At the same time, two Jesuit psychologists were taking the drug for research purposes at the UCLA medical center under the direction of clinical psychologist Ed Maupin. They gave a talk to our community describing their experiences. All I remember is one of them saying that the drug began to have its effects while he was lying face down on a hospital bed. The bed suddenly became the universe and he, her lover; the two joined in cosmic bliss. He said the experience left him with a profound sense of the meaning of Christ's becoming embodied and how being a priest giving the sacraments was taking part in a ritual of mystical love.

Intrigued by those hints, I soon took LSD with a Jesuit friend in the midst of an eight-day retreat. I experienced the kinds of things that have been well, and usually tediously, documented: heaven and hell, the universe in a grain of sand, the unity of inner and outer.

It brought about a major change in my sense of *body* and *spirit*. I found myself only beginning a slight movement of my hips to get up out of my chair, and in that movement I was overwhelmed by layers upon layers of experiences ranging from the bare feeling of muscle and bone, memories of early childhood toilet training, to scenes from James Joyce's *Ulysses*, to the transcendental logic of Immanuel Kant, to the bare peace (or terror or love) devoid of content, spoken of by Ignatius. Each of those images was accompanied by feelings whose intensities were magnified to such an extent that I could not mistake what they were: unspeakable terror, lush sexual desire, joy beyond my imaginings. The images, ideas and feeling were not separated but were instead deeply embedded in that simple hip rotation. As I got used to these effects, I began to experiment. I would take a deep breath, setting off feelings of ribs opening, lungs pulsing as I took in air, visions of angels and demons fighting through those costal gates, the angels winning, and preparing my bronchioles for an orgastic inspiration of the Holy Spirit.

Shortly after that trip in 1967, I was drawn to go to the newly formed Esalen Institute in Big Sur whose brochure said that people there were discussing the relationships among Eastern and Western mysticism, LSD and transformation of the body. Michael Murphy, its founder, was interested in the relationship between body therapies and transformations of consciousness. Like Father Healy, he had a deep interest in the extraordinary physical phenomena recorded in the lives of the saints—levitation, elongation, fragrant smells of long-dead, unembalmed corpses. At a weekend seminar, for which I received academic credit towards a master's degree in theology at the Jesuit Alma College, I heard philosopher of religion Huston Smith talk about his LSD experiences at Harvard with Timothy Leary and Richard Alpert and how those experiences were related to ancient mystical traditions in Asia. I also participated in encounter groups lead by Will Schutz, and t'ai chi classes led by a refugee Shanghai banker, Gia Fu Feng. I could sense that here were paths on which I could travel through the layers of my experience until I reached those primal places where I could eventually trust my own experience. Yet, I shrunk in fear, walled up inside, as I found myself for the first time in my life naked with men and women in the baths, with women brushing against me, smiling, inviting. While my Jesuit companion spent his nights with one of those friendly women while others danced on the terrace to drumbeats, I withdrew to our cabin and read Huston Smith's book on world religions.

Gia Fu invited me to visit his meditation retreat, which was just a mile above Alma on the summit of the Santa Cruz mountains. I hiked up there in the dark one morning, arriving an hour before sunrise when his group began its meditation. He welcomed me warmly, escorted me into a glassed-in room facing directly east towards Mount Loma Prieta and briefly explained that I should simply sit comfortably erect on a cushion—but cross-legged, a double Arsenius according to Father Healy's teaching!—and pay attention to my breathing. During that hour of conscious sitting and breathing, the insights, images and feelings generated by having meditated thousands of hours during eleven years descended into my skin and lungs from their remote home in some distant mind. I felt once again the naive contemplative sense I had known as a child and young adolescent, yet given density by years of sitting in bleakness.

Breathing, to my surprise, was not just breathing; nor sitting just sitting.

❦

THAT COMBINATION OF meditating on subtle impulses, philosophically sifting through layers of desire, and the psychedelic breakdown of the division between inner self and outer world prompted me to wonder about a differently organized, less hierarchical world. What would it be like if parents and teachers nurtured the native curiosity of children instead of squeezing them into procrustean categories of thought? If the supple mobility of those children were encouraged in the classroom instead of being considered a threat to discipline and serious thought? If compassionate touch became more common than torture and killing; if women and the aging were truly respected; if animals, forests, water and air were cared for—what then would we make of *body* and *spirit?*

6

Vertical Enlightenment: Ida Rolf

In my slowly forming vision of a non-authoritarian society, I tended to think that religious dogmatism was the main barrier preventing its realization. When I eventually left the Jesuits in 1970, I assumed that I was entering a more democratic and empirically driven world, a mistake I made in common with many social thinkers who argued that secularism would be the key to realizing the West's twenty-five-hundred-year-old dream of such a community. We now see that Nazism and the various Communisms surpass the extremes of medieval Catholicism and Islam in their suppression of the human spirit. As I became more involved in a secular life, I came to realize that religious dogmas are not the only obstacles to genuine democracy.

I got the chance to witness the minutest details of why it is so hard to create democratic social structures among a group of body-workers, "Rolfers," with whom I was intimately involved in the founding moments of a new institution. As one of the first students of Ida Rolf and a director on the board of her new organization, I had the privilege of seeing the emergence of a formal political and theoretical system from more primal, experimental processes. I was able to grasp how freeing one's rib cage for breathing or creating more flexibility in one's spinal column facilitates spiritual transformation. At the same time, I saw how confusion about *body* and *spirit*, combined with a lack of modesty, can give rise to an exclusive claim to truth and create yet another authoritarian enclave within the fragmented commonweal.

In 1969, my final year in the Jesuits, I had gone to Yale to complete my doctoral studies in philosophy. Rev. William Sloane Coffin, the university chaplain indicted along with Dr. Spock and my fellow Jesuit Father Dan Berrigan for anti-war activities, invited me to be his assistant pastor and chaplain of the graduate school. I used my budget to bring to staid New Haven the rag-a-tag band of practitioners who were gathering at Esalen doing sensory awareness, bioenergetics, group encounter and psychodrama. What interested me the most was Structural Integration, nicknamed "Rolfing" after its founder.

The effects on my life of the first session of that work rivaled those of my Thanksgiving experience in the Pittsburgh Cathedral. It occurred in a small cold room of Dwight Hall, the chaplain's building on the Yale Quad, at the hands of Ed Maupin, the former UCLA psychologist who had given my Jesuit friends LSD.

During that first hour, Ed moved his fingers slowly and deeply within my pectoral muscles, penetrating right to the surface of the ribs. I went into a state of terror accompanied by the most intense pain that I had ever experienced. I feared that his fingers would pierce through my rib cage, which felt like a hollow eggshell, and I would die. He encouraged me to pay attention to my breathing. I suddenly discovered the fullness of my chest, its liquids, organs, pulsing lungs. I was overcome with feelings of liberation from the old bonds of asthma and fears of hell. He inserted his elbow deep into the rotator muscles of my hips, causing an even more excruciating pain. As I breathed and relaxed into the sensations, I found myself flooded again with memories from my past of how I had collapsed under pressure, giving into people, afraid of what they would do to me. In a second session he moved his knuckles deeply into the sole of my foot which I had imagined was like the leather sole on my shoes. Again, excruciating pain. Then the ecstasy of feeling layer upon layer of muscles and memories in that small place. I stood and felt a strength that I had never known. In a third session, he moved his fingers deeply into the quadratus lumborum muscle that spans from the twelfth rib to the top of the pelvis. For an instant, I thought I would pass out from the pain and terror. Then again, as I breathed, I felt in my muscular reactions to his fingers countless memories of a typical pattern in which my first reaction to challenges or new ideas from my friends and parents would be "no," a refusal to let what they were saying enter me, followed by a later "yes," when they had already been put off by my resistance.

At the end of each session, he dug his knuckles and elbows deep into the tissues surrounding my spinal column. To my shock, for a few moments I felt a movement in my vertebrae that I had never known. I got a fleeting glimpse that there is such a thing as spinal movement, in contrast to which I realized that I had been congenitally stiff.

Those sessions with Ed clarified what I had intuited on my first LSD trips: that matters of the spirit as well as memories, emotions and ideas are embedded in muscle, intestine and lungs. They are not separate *things*, but layers of the self, like the successive civilizations archaeologists unearth on a dig at an ancient mound. In the precise moment of feeling his elbow in my gluteal muscles, I could focus on a sharp physical pain, or the memory of my father's anger, or the bliss of merging with cosmic forces. They were all there in that single instant.

Moreover, I became aware of more radical possibilities of change than I had ever imagined, even when I was inspired by the idea of converting a heathen world to Christ. It is hard to express how dramatic an experience it is to sense that a vertebra or a chronically stressed group of muscles, which seem to be an indubitably permanent facet of life, can actually be altered. The sense is that if my seemingly solid bones and decades-old muscular tensions can change, then certainly my less substantial moods, fleeting patterns of desire, let alone the flimsy structures of politics, can also change.

By 1970, I HAD BEEN expelled from the Jesuits and excommunicated by the Church for having married Elissa Melamed, a thirty-eight-year-old divorced mother of three young children, Mike, Mora and Rina. She had a long past as a political radical, educated at Manhattan's High School of Music and Art, where she had been a member of the Jewish Marxist organization, Hashomer Hatzair. She had been a Phi Beta Kappa at Radcliffe and had earned her M.A. at Harvard, where she had married a psychiatrist whom she had divorced the year before I met her. She had been a student of modern dance since high school, and in recent years had become a consultant in the Connecticut public school system where she taught teachers how to use body movement to enhance the interest of their students.

Our first three meetings, which resulted in our living together, set the tone of our fourteen-year marriage. We first met at a wedding that John Steinbeck, III, then a Buddhist monk, and I performed on a raft in the middle of a pond for members of an artists' commune at a Connecticut country house. Rina and Mora were the flower girls. Elissa and I danced for hours, stoned on LSD-seasoned punch. The next time I met her was at a workshop I sponsored as Yale Graduate School chaplain, given by a man who was posing as an Esalen group leader (he turned out to have been a cook in the Esalen kitchen). She and an African-American drummer led us in an evening of nude body movement by firelight in the Gothic wooden-paneled room of one of Yale's old buildings. The third and charmed meeting happened after a seminar with Ram Dass, whom I had invited to spend a week at Yale. She telephoned me at seven o'clock the next morning to say that Ram Dass had made her realize how empty her life felt. I went over to talk with her, we instantly fell in love and I moved in with her and her children a few days later. After a life of celibacy and living alone always with my own room, I suddenly found myself in my first long-term sexual relationship, surrounded by three young children. I didn't even take any time to reflect on what difficulties I might have to deal with.

78

❀

As I entered this unfamiliar life of lover and father and continued to complete my graduate studies in philosophy at Yale, I became struck by the contrast between on the one hand, the lush feelings of sexuality with Elissa and the visionary fervor of the fledgling Rolfing community, and, on the other, the staleness of academia. Elissa and I began to imagine what it would be like for me to give up philosophy for a career in Rolfing and for her to develop her practice as a teacher of body movement. We envisioned moving somewhere closer to nature and using our skills to support ourselves on travels throughout the world.

Elissa, whose severe back pain had forced her to give up her career in modern dance, was at that time being "processed" (the odd word commonly used to describe being Rolfed) by Ida Rolf's son Dick Demmerle in New York. One day she happened to meet Ida in the waiting room and asked her what she thought about my becoming her student. "Sounds like an ectomorphic intellectual," she said. "They never make good Rolfers. But send him down anyhow and we'll have a look." When I arrived at her Riverside Drive apartment, her home and Dick's New York office, Dr. Rolf and her secretary Rosemary Feitis were fretting about how to rebut an attack on her work that had just appeared in the magazine section of the Sunday *New York Times*. They interviewed me over a cup of tea, our conversation punctuated by Elissa's screams from the next room. I tried to impress Dr. Rolf with my Yale credentials and my experience of teaching philosophy. She looked bored until she finally pried out of me the confession that I had been a Jesuit. Then, for reasons still unclear to me, her eyes lit up and she agreed to train me. As I rose to leave she looked at my body very carefully and asked, with an irritated tone, who my Rolfer was. "Oh him," she sighed, "Ed Maupin just can't get the head on top of the body!"

At that meeting, Ida was seventy years old. She had the body of one who has spent her life doing hard physical labor, short and stocky, muscular arms and shoulders. The long fingers on her immense hands were gnarled and arthritic, her shoulders stooped. I would later hear her poignantly complain that because of her curved body, she had never been able to experience "Rolf consciousness." Despite her severe weathering by work and age, I found her strikingly beautiful. She had long white hair pulled up on the top of her head with a silver barrette and a white rose, with a Navajo silver necklace and many silver rings. She was wearing a cashmere sweater and expensively tailored slacks. She had a hard time getting up out of her rocking chair to say goodbye.

The first stage of my Rolfing training was a six-week session during the summer of 1971 in a small house Ida had rented on the Big Sur cliffs, a mile north of Esalen. As in all the early training classes, most of the students were middle-aged people whose lives, like mine, had been plunged into disarray during the 1960s by encounter groups, Gestalt therapy, psychedelic drugs and political activism. We had come in our campers from all over the United States seeking in Dr. Rolf a way of living in the world that fit our new sense of the importance of the body and of a more inclusive spirituality. This particular class of some twenty people, six of whom were in their final stages of being prepared to practice Rolfing, included a Cambridge philosopher, a concert flautist, a cardiologist, a neurophysiologist, the actor who for ten years had played the sheriff on "Bonanza," a former Miss Florida, an ex-NASA engineer, a poet, a weaver, a Mormon elder, a biologist from the Salk Institute, a Danish fashion designer and a former symphony orchestra conductor from Julliard.

The daily training sessions went from early morning until sundown, with Ida setting the pace, demonstrating her work for several hours with people who had come from as far as Hawaii, Toronto and Maine in the hope of being healed by her from diseases and structural anomalies that mainstream medical treatments had failed to cure. I watched a twenty-eight-year-old woman diagnosed as a spastic from birth begin to walk for the first time in her life. The blood pressure of a sixty-five-year-old politician with hypertension reduced each day until it reached normal. A retired Air Force colonel, disabled by an accident during a tour of duty, began to use his arms for the first time in twelve years. Lost color-vision was restored, arthritis disappeared, complaints about impotence and constipation ceased.

❦

THE DETAILS OF HOW Ida came to develop her method illustrate how creativity and rigidity can mix in a given tradition and weaken its healing capacities. Her story lies within the pragmatic context of a peculiarly American tradition of healing by manipulating a person's skeleton and connective tissues. An original pioneer was Dr. Andrew Still, a Missouri physician, abolitionist and champion of women's suffrage. Shortly after the Civil War, he watched three of his children die of spinal meningitis, unable to help them with his medical expertise. He began a series of experiments, some working with the skeletons of exhumed Indians, which resulted in his creating what we now know as osteopathy. Still founded the first osteopathic college in Kirksville, Missouri, in 1892. Three years later, another popular form of healing, chiropractic, evolved out of experiments made by Dr. Daniel Palmer on relieving headaches and hearing deficiencies by creating space within the spinal column.

Ida spent nearly fifty years of her professional life within the community of osteopaths and chiropractors. Her first encounter with that work occurred when she was a young adult on a camping trip to the Rockies in 1916 after graduating from Barnard College. While she was tying up her gear one afternoon, her horse kicked her. The next day she developed pneumonia. Within a very short time her breathing became so impaired and her fever so severe that she had to be taken to a small Montana town for help. To her surprise, the doctor prescribed a treatment from the local osteopath. After a simple manipulation of her spine, her fever was immediately reduced and her breathing became normal. She was able to return to her family's Long Island home. While there, she continued having treatments in Port Jefferson with a blind osteopath, Dr. Morrison, until she had fully recovered.

The Montana osteopath's simple act of adjusting her spine was to have a lifelong impact on her conceptions of healing. It dramatically convinced her of the truth of the basic osteopathic principle enunciated by Andrew Still that structure determines function. The vertical alignment of the head, rib cage, pelvis and legs can radically affect health, behavior and consciousness. From that time on, she continued to receive hands-on work from these practitioners and to study their work.

During those same years, she embarked on a lifelong study of spiritual practices which were on the fringes of mainstream American culture. While she was a graduate student in biochemistry at Columbia she studied with a tantric yogi in Nyack. Through him, she began to wonder about the connection between the osteopathic notion of vertical skeletal alignment and the ancient notion of the alignment of chakras. She would eventually synthesize certain ideas of Western biology and Eastern spirituality into the notion that access to the furthest reaches of the human potential required removal of the muscular torsions and skeletal imbalances impeding the free flow of various energies such as oxygen, lymph, blood and neural messengers.

Her father's death in 1928 left her an inheritance large enough to free her from the need to work for a living. She began a lifetime of world travel, studying various spiritual and physical disciplines. She spent several months in Geneva studying homeopathy. She traveled to London to study the work of F. Matthias Alexander. While there she joined John Bennett's Gurdjieff group, an esoteric spiritual community which put her in contact with some of the well-known people who would later become her patients, like Greta Garbo and Georgia O'Keefe. She studied the method of posture training developed by Bess Mensendieck, which was eventually adopted by several prominent East coast secondary schools and private universities. She joined Korzybski's General Semantics Movement whose early members included Gregory Bateson, Margaret Mead and Charlotte Selver.

In her continued studies of osteopathy, she became particularly inspired by the work of Still's early associate William Sutherland. In working with his patients, Sutherland chanced upon the discovery that very subtle manipulations of their cranial and sacral bones had far-reaching effects on their health and their spiritual consciousness. He pursued these investigations and developed an elaborate set of strategies for practicing the work. Although this highly refined hands-on tradition has virtually disappeared from formal osteopathic training, it has been preserved and evolved in the teaching of a few osteopaths who have remained true to their origins. Most Rolfers today are intimately involved with this work.[23] (I have had ecstatic experiences that are nearly as pleasurable as orgasms, along with significant relief of my chronic back pain, when such a practitioner is doing these gentle small movements on my cranium.)

For several years, Ida often practiced what she was learning on her family and friends. But she confined herself to teaching yoga postures and movement exercises. In 1940, a series of events set her in the direction of developing a unified system of physical manipulation. She married an engineer named Demmerle who died as a young man and about whom she said very little, except on occasion how much she loved him. They had two sons, Alan and Dick, whom she raised by herself. She would say that they were born with certain "structural difficulties," but she remained vague about their exact nature. In one account, she said that one of her sons had a skull that was "too narrow." In another, she wrote that as a child Dick "had an anterior dorsal and a posterior lumbar spine ... a typical 'soft' body."[24] She tried to find help for them from several people, with little success. She resorted to doing the job herself. While teaching us the Recipe for the "sixth hour" of her work, she told us of a time when she had taken Alan and Dick to the circus in Manhattan. At the end of the long day they boarded the train for Long Island. The boys, then four and six, were restless and cranky. Having learned from her Nyack yoga teacher techniques for manipulating the anus, associated with the first chakra, she rubbed Dick's and Alan's and happily found the children calmed. Ida continued to work on Alan and Dick and her daughters-in-law and grandchildren until her last years. I have warm memories of Ida sitting in the evenings on her porch at Pigeon Key lovingly kneading Dick's hands and wrists, swollen from working all day in our training classes.

When Alan and Dick were old enough to begin school, Ida heard about the case of a woman named Ethel. Ethel had taught music at the Ethical Culture Center in New York until she had tripped on a hole in the sidewalk and fallen. She could no longer use her hands, even to do the simplest of actions like combing her hair. Ida, then investigating the school for her boys, offered to work on her with the agreement that if the work were successful, Ethel would give the boys piano lessons. In four sessions, Ethel was able to play again. Soon she had recovered enough to be able to enlist in the wartime WACs.

In 1942, Ida traveled to Glendale, California to study with the osteopath Dr. Amy Cochran. Aside from being a well-known healer with a following in New York, Dr. Cochran was also said to be the psychic channel for Benjamin Rush, the physician who signed the Declaration of Independence. The day Ida returned home from Glendale, she called her friend Grace, a forty-five-year-old woman who had been crippled in an accident when she was eight years old. "I said Grace, we're getting to work and we're going to fix you up. The day I started working with Grace was the day I really got Rolfing going. I would look at her and say, 'This is in the wrong place,' and I'd say, 'Now, Grace, does this feel better this way, or does it feel better in the other direction?' And she'd say, 'That way,' so we'd organize that corner. This went on for a couple of years, and in the end Grace picked herself up and went to California all by herself. That was when the first principle of Rolfing was really born—moving the soft tissue toward the place where it really belongs."[25]

Ida was describing an activity where she is using her fingers, fists and elbows to move the person's connective tissues — fascia, tendons, ligaments and muscle groups. The manipulation is slow and often extremely deep, the fingers going all the way through the abdomen, for example, to touch the psoas muscle which lies directly in front of the spinal column. Or behind the hard into the soft palate of the mouth, even up into the nasal passages. Unlike massage, which aims at relaxing and evoking pleasant sensations, each move described by Ida is aimed at making specific changes in the tissues, sometimes accompanied by pain.

For a decade Ida continued to work with people who happened to present themselves at her doorstep. In the early 1950s, when she got her first opportunity to teach formally, she began to formulate her thirty years of experimentation into a communicable technique. This occurred after a General Semantics seminar in the Berkshires where she met Sam Fulkerson, a vitamin distributor whose ribs had been broken and teeth knocked out in a recent auto accident. Impressed by the results of Ida's work with him, he promoted a series of week-long seminars given by her for chiropractors and osteopaths throughout the United States. She began to develop a reputation, and articles about her method began to appear in osteopathic journals. She complained, however, that these practitioners were failing to grasp her integrated vision of human evolution; they were simply taking pieces of her teaching and fitting them into their techniques of physical manipulation.

Still, Sutherland and Palmer began with a holistic vision that caught Ida's imagination. Alexander Still, is often quoted as saying: "The body is its own pharmacy," meaning that the distribution of its own healing compounds is a function of proper alignment of body parts, effected by direct manipulation of connective tissues. William Sutherland was a student of the biological mystic Immanuel Swedenborg. He considered that physical manipulations were directly related to profound changes in consciousness.

And yet by the time that Ida began teaching, the education of osteopaths and chiropractors had come under the sway of the bio-medical establishment, where the governing paradigm defines *body* as a mechanical system governed exclusively by the laws of the natural sciences, unrelated to *soul* or *spirit*. She found it difficult to find students within that world who were capable of responding to her vision in more than a superficial technical way of "learning new moves."

Ida had come to a radically non-dualistic view of the person in which *body* and *spirit* signified not different parts of the person, but something like different layers of energy or refinement. For her, touching the tissues of the body was to touch the spirit of a person. From her early twenties, she thought of the upright body balanced in the field of gravity as a spiritual body. The development of the so-called psychological and spiritual capacities of freedom, love and wisdom were part and parcel of cultivating neuromuscular balance in response to the earth's field. For her, as for Wilhelm Reich, F. Matthias Alexander and Elsa Gindler, one's personality is embedded in the interweavings of muscle fibers, bony torsions and halting gait.

She eventually was driven to create her own institution, at first training only a handful of associates including her son, Dick, and a movement specialist, Dorothy Nolte. In 1965, Dorothy was in Los Angeles attending a lecture by Fritz Perls, the founder of Gestalt Therapy. He had been given six months to live because of a serious heart condition. Dorothy offered to give him a session which so dramatically improved his condition that he invited Ida herself to Esalen Institute to work on him. The success of her sub-sequent work with Perls made her one of the most popular fig-ures in the Human Potential Movement. At the request of many people, she soon began teaching groups who would identify them-selves as Rolfers. The first class was held in a room at the Presidio Motel in San Francisco on six weekends. The students were psy-chiatrist Jack Downing, Bernie Gunther, an athletic coach and popularizer of Charlotte Selver's Sensory Awareness work, and Robert Hall, also a psychiatrist who would soon create the Lomi

School, a synthesis of manipulative work, Gestalt therapy, meditation and the martial arts.

Under pressure to teach neophytes in brief workshop formats, Ida integrated her fifty years of experimentation into a very simple and reasonable theory:

1. Consider the body as an aggregate of large segments of weight (head, thorax, abdomen, pelvis, legs, feet) moving in the field of gravity.
2. The relationships among the segments (a person's unique body structure) are a function of balance and tension in the connective tissues that bind the segments into a unity.
3. Those tissues — fascia, tendons, ligaments and muscle groups — are plastic, capable of radical change.
4. The direction of this change can be either in the direction of entropy due to aging and trauma, or, through sensitive manipulation and educated self-awareness, in the direction of balance and harmony with the vertical field of gravity.

Rolfing mysticism unfolded from the fourth point. In brief moments after my work with Ed Maupin, and then more permanently as I made this work my central practice, I began to enjoy the peculiar experience that draws so many people to Rolfing. While sitting, standing or walking I found myself in a deep sense of peace and connectedness with the world about me. It is hard to speak of. It is as if, in a certain sense, my ego's pretensions felt properly dwarfed in relation to the vast field of the earth. It was precisely that sense of peace, not all the miraculous cures, that interested Ida. It frustrated her that we and others became more occupied with the cures. She complained again and again until the very end of her life that virtually no one, not even those closest to her, had appreciated that her work was not primarily about the direct relief of physical symptoms but about initiating people into harmonious spiritual consciousness, which in her view coincides with having vertically aligned body segments. Eliminating the primary sources of illness, she argued, could only come about by that structural transformation of consciousness.

Ida's is a contemporary version of ancient non-dualistic traditions in which the relationship between the physical and the spiritual is linked to the upright posture, the uniquely human standpoint. The notion of uprightness crosses spiritual, ethnic and physical boundaries. Western Christianity embodies that ideal in its Gothic art and architecture where the lifting off from the earth is associated with sanctity. It appears in the ancient practices of t'ai chi chu'an where the movement down through the legs and up through the head produce the sense of wholeness associated with contacting the Tao. The complex *asanas* of hatha yoga aim at producing a vertical spine associated with the desired state of samadhi. The complex Tantric practices are designed to bring the various energy centers, chakras, into harmonious vertical alignment. Native American rituals constantly embody the twofold movement down into the earth, upwards towards the sky.

Ida often quoted the words of Suzuki Roshi replying to a student who asked if the proper sitting posture is a means to enlightenment: "These forms are not the means of obtaining the right state of mind. To take this posture is itself to have the right state of mind."[26] In a similar vein, the master of a particular form of Japanese poems structured around thirty-one syllables called *waka* writes: "In composing *waka,* one should prepare oneself to assume the correct posture. If one becomes accustomed to composing in an unrestrained posture such as standing or lying down, one cannot compose at all on formal occasions.... My father admonished me not to compose *waka* even for a short while without the correct sitting posture."[27]

Ida's four-point synthesis was eminently sensible and effective. It was abstract enough so that it, like Freud's theory of the unconscious or Reich's theory of the bioenergetic core of personality, had the potential to generate a wide variety of methods and inquiries. But, as with many such generative ideas, the seeds of authoritarianism were there, too. Ida had set herself the impossible task of communicating fifty years of experience in two six-week periods to people like myself who knew virtually nothing about the body or about manipulation. We were sent forth from these brief twelve weeks to carry her message to the ends of the earth, treating people with severe emotional and physical disorders. It's not surprising, then, that she would feel compelled to reduce her imaginative experimentalism to simple maps that were easy to follow, the kinds of maps that rapidly turn into simplistic dogmas. There were two: "The Template" or "Rolf Line" and "The Recipe."

The Template or The Line was a geometrical map of Ida's ideal body structure, indicating the precise location of the head and neck, torso, pelvis, legs and feet. Ida had been inspired by the general notion of the ideal of a vertically aligned body as early as her studies with the Tantric yogi in Nyack. In her early years of teaching, she spoke only very generally of a body whose segments were so vertically aligned that standing in the field of gravity would not cause undue tensions on the muscles and ligaments which bound them together.

She defined her ideal by contrast to others. She faulted the Western anatomic model of normality for having lumbar and cervical curves which were too pronounced. The spinal curves aimed at by practitioners of t'ai chi chu'an and F. M. Alexander work were too flat, she said, and the zazen posture threw the sacrum forward. During the 1970s, as she worked with an artist-Rolfer on illustrations for her book,[28] she tried to define her ideal more precisely. As with her method of working, her way of defining this ideal was radically experimental. She observed the people with whom she had worked successfully over a long period of time and tried to extrapolate from the changes in their bodies where they would end up if she was perfectly satisfied with them.

A typical instance of how she went about sculpting her ideal occurred one day in our Big Sur class when a student asked her exactly what she meant by the "horizontal pelvis" that was supposed to be the aim of our work. She asked us to strip to our underwear and lined us up according to what she judged to be our degree of structural perfection. Then she had two of her assistants go to each of us, one putting his finger on the top of the pubic bone, the other on the tailbone or coccyx. We discovered that as they progressed along her line of excellence, an imaginary vector between the top of the pubic bone and the second of the three coccygeal bodies in the tail bone moved towards the horizontal. Many years later, that suggestive empirical observation of a minuscule random population had become the definition of the ideal structure of the pelvis, guiding the way Rolfers are taught to see, work and give movement instructions.

The Recipe is a map of how to "process" people in ten sessions, so that they will move well along the way towards the territory mapped by the Template. Each session has a definite structural goal, described in relation to specific anatomical groups. The second session, for example, concentrates primarily on the feet and legs; the fourth, on the adductor muscles of the thighs; the seventh, on the head and neck. At times, she even detailed how the practitioner is to hold and move his or her hands while doing a particular session: for the fifth session, for example, she told us to keep our hands together, flat out, fingers moving up to catch the edges of the abdominal muscles, wrists dropping, lifting the tissue.

Ida herself worked very idiosyncratically, as with Ethel and Grace, responding to the unique problems presented by her patients and experimenting with different ways of handling them, always observing the results, getting feedback from the person, and frequently modifying what she was doing. I saw her do first sessions on people's feet, elbows and tongues, areas that the Recipe enjoined us from touching during that particular session.

Ida was not unaware of the problems created by teaching in such a formulaic manner. She said that the goal of the advanced class for Rolfers was to "transcend the mechanicalness of the Recipe." In a lecture to her Institute about that training she told us: "A 'recipe' is fine—it works as everyone of you has reason to know. But when you get to be a 'chef' instead of a 'cook' you create your results not by a recipe but by your recognition of the interplay of food and nutritional values and materials." It is easier to see the likenesses among people and to work on them in the same way, she would say, than it is to see their radical individuality and to tailor our work to that distinctiveness.

The transformation of the experimentally derived notions of the Recipe and Template into fixed dogma disturbingly reminded me, when I encountered it, of the tangled web of *body, spirit* and authority in which I had lived as a Jesuit. The Rolf ideas, like the dogma of the Holy Trinity and the "Rules of Modesty," gave us the exhilarating sense that our work had a transcendent purpose, and that we were superior to other physical manipulators. Like all peoples cut off from their ancient roots, we hungered for ritual and a common spiritual language, which is exactly what the Recipe and the Template provided. At the beginning of the 1970s, we were all mavericks, living on the edges of society, in a time of tremendous cultural upheaval. I can't think of a single Rolfer, including Ida and Dick, who maintained regular ties with a mainstream American church or synagogue. We were looking in many directions for something that would fill that spiritual vacuum: various schools of Buddhism, shamanism, the cults of Da Free John, Gurdjieff, Rajneesh, Ichazo, Muktananda, Werner Erhard and other psychic and spiritist movements. In my own case, after thirty-five years of feeling that I was in the vanguard of a movement that was preparing the world for a millennium of peace and justice, it would be difficult to accept the fact that I was a member of only one among many communities doing a modest bit to better the human lot.

The non-empirical exclusivity of Ida's pretensions came more to the fore during the final years of her life when she began to make several statements to the effect that her life's goal was the creation of a superior race of humans by means of imposing the Template on a small and elite population. In one of her final letters to the Institute she wrote the following passage, whose megalomania was hard to gloss over: "Rolfing is being accepted as one of the most basic, one of the most reliable means of developing whatever potential is latent in any given human, psychological as well as physical. It is possible that we are seeing here the first conscious attempt at evolution made by any species in modern times."[29] She and many Rolfers began to speak of The Line in the same way that members of spiritual communities speak of satori or grace. With her encouragement, we began speaking of ourselves as heirs of the esoteric traditions of gnosticism and alchemy. Looking for historical antecedents, Ida and her teachers scanned reproductions of Egyptian art for instances of the Template. Figures on temple walls looked vaguely like Rolfers at work. One young Rolfer went to Egypt to search out evidence for the origins of the Template. To his credit, he acknowledged that he found none.

There was even the evolution of a priesthood. Until 1972, Ida personally interviewed each candidate and did all the training. With this scheme, she could only accept eighteen students a year. As the demand for Rolfers rapidly increased, she ordained two creative Rolfers as official teachers. In spite of their excellence and that of the handful she picked in later years, she made a crucial decision for determining the future of her heritage. She appointed these teachers *in perpetuo*, with no term of office or outside system of checks and balances. Soon formed into the education committee of the Institute, they were granted the exclusive right to select additional teachers. Their function was to protect the integrity of Rolfing, to see that its transmission was uncontaminated. They soon came to be known as "the keepers of the faith."

By 1974, a fully articulated secular church had been created. It had a dogma in the form of the Recipe and Template, a detailed map of transforming the world, a carefully structured initiation process, and a priestly body charged with decisions concerning orthodoxy. There was even an organ of censorship, the Publication Committee charged with approving the content of any materials published which might affect the reputation of the Institute. These basic structures are still in place with senior members of the Institute continuing to argue whether or not it is permissible to depart from the Recipe and Template and whether teachers should be subject to the democratic checks and balances of the community of practitioners. Another ironical ecclesiastical parallel occurred while I was writing this book, when the two men originally ordained by Ida as teachers became the Luther and Calvin of Rolfing, leaving the Institute with the charge that it had departed from the mystical ideals of its founder. They created their Protestant "Guild for Structural Integration."

🍃

DESPITE ITS PROBLEMS, the Rolfing community continued to inspire me because of its common vision. It is hard to describe what it was like to share with a small group of people the surprising new sense of balance, ease of movement and deep sexual release, let alone the altered states of consciousness that are the unique results of Rolfing. In 1970, when few people had even heard of such kinds of deep body work, it was even more difficult than now to find people who knew those experiences. So it was a relief to be with those who did. And there was the genuine desire to share those marvelous experiences with others, feeling that the world would be in better shape if more people could feel what we did.

At the same time, my years in that community left me in fundamentally the same place I was left by my religious training, puzzled about the ownership of my soul, feeling still imprisoned within the cage of the double bind. Here the conflicts were recast in somatic terms. Like Father Healy, Ida constantly pressed me to pay attention to my experience, both to the course of inner events and to what my eyes and touch told me about other people. But at the same time, she complained that virtually no one had been successful in embodying the Template which alone would give the authorized kinds of experiences associated with truth. She said that my defective body structure with its ankylosing spinal column precluded even the possibility of my attaining that experience. I felt humiliated.

Her collapsing of *spirit* into *body* perpetuated the double bind, giving me a deep appreciation for the liberating aspects of Cartesian dualism, despite all its problems. Our belief that a precise structuring of the head and neck was identical with spiritual consciousness kept us enmeshed in the autocratic form of Ida's teaching and the hierarchical nature of her organization. Both Rolfing and the Catholic Church brought the two extreme poles on the continuum of experience too close together. Failing to locate and refine other landmarks on that continuum made it difficult to gain access to crucial experiences which might transform debilitating conflicts into growth-inducing paradoxes.

For example, there is the luminescent region of experience that we associate with *mind;* it originates in the child's wonder about the world. If nurtured, it develops into the kind of inquisitive spirit that raises the uncomfortable questions which true believers try to ignore. It unfolds in philosophy and the sciences, which work methodically to pare away from human opinion its accretions of dogma and bias. Ida did not encourage that spirit. She often sarcastically dismissed the admission of a student that he or she could not see the changes in a person with whom Ida was working or a puzzle about an idea that Ida was explaining. Although she professed an interest in scientific research, it was not in the spirit of exploring the unknown and whittling away at unexamined claims but more a matter of public relations, proving to the public what she already assumed to be true.

There is also the layer of experience labeled *"psyche,"* the murky region of emotions and unconscious processes revealed in dreams, tics, fantasies, hallucinations and slips of the tongue. Like my Jesuit superiors, Ida often tried to discredit that area. She had little patience for people who broke into tears during a session or who expressed a memory of long-forgotten feelings about a past injury. She urged us to move on without giving any importance to such personal expressions. Failing to take seriously those layers of experience, we and other Somatic practitioners too readily assumed that what we perceived in someone else was true, without realizing that we were often seeing and touching our own projections.

In Ida I had the opportunity to observe the details of what I had glimpsed only from a distance in the founders of Catholicism and the Jesuits: how people with a compassionate desire to create a better life for others become infected by the virus of an inflated pretension that they know what no one else knows. Until the very end of her life, I was moved by her empathy with suffering human beings and her passion for introducing common sense into our lives. I often cried when I watched her work lovingly with a crippled child or an aged arthritic. I was thrilled when she spoke of her vision of a more peaceful world. And yet I saw how the modest and effective way in which she had restored Ethel's use of her hands or Grace's ability to walk and had given Fritz Perls extra years of life became distorted into an inflated dream of shaping a new humanity on the basis of her idiosyncratic vision alone.

I saw myself reflected in her. Along with my deep conviction about the genius inherent in all people and my commitment to shape institutions to foster respect for that genius, has been the ever-present temptation to think that I, and a few like-minded others, have a privileged access to the Truth. That is why I was more entrapped by the Recipe and Template than many of my colleagues who had a less authoritarian background and a more cavalier attitude towards the Rolfing process. For nearly a decade, I followed the Recipe with great success; I had a succession of gratifying experiences with clients ranging from infants to people in their eighties who had all kinds of problems—physical, psychological and spiritual. But I continued to have the feeling I had had since adolescence that I was imprisoning myself without knowing how to break out. The chronic spinal pain that had been relieved by Ed Maupin was replaced by a new and even more intense network of pain that came from long days of working my fingers, knuckles and elbows deeply into people's bodies and from repeated attempts to fit my spinal column into the procrustean Template.

SECTION II

Body-Spirit Ecosystems

THE ROMAN CATHOLIC CHURCH, the Jesuits and Rolfing are identifiable institutions, with buildings and documented conditions for membership. Each has notions of body, spirit, and authority which are clearly defined in official texts, along with formal techniques for shaping members to embody those notions. We can date beginnings and endings of membership in them. There are, however, more ancient and powerful forces carving out the outlines of any particular viewpoint just as long-established patterns of wind, rain and temperature variations promote local flora and fauna. Unlike churches and schools of therapy, these forces offer us no choice but to live within them. They are so much a part of our everyday lives that we easily come to feel that their relentless pressures are natural. They are as difficult to change as the weather.

Ethnicity, sociopolitics and gender are three such primal fronts. In my case, they shaped me to feel that only a narrow spectrum of white men had access to a universal voice which had the capacity, even the moral obligation, to speak for all other people.

Between Cultures

I WAS ALWAYS vaguely aware of the peculiarities of "white Euro-American" consciousness, although it took me decades to grasp how deeply it affected my perception of "reality." Growing up in a working class neighborhood in downtown Sacramento, I had Black, Hispanic and Jewish friends, while my parents' friends were exclusively white Christians. When I was still a young child, I was puzzled and hurt when my father and his friends made snide cracks about niggers, pachucos and kikes.

In the religious world, I found a lively debate about the difference between cultural variations and a transcendent human nature, the Church priding itself on being *kat-holikos,* for the whole, valid for everyone, "whether Jew or Greek, man or woman, free or slave." Because the stories of Christianity were embedded in the particularities of Semitic and Romance languages and Mediterranean imagery, religious scholars devoted serious efforts to developing critical methods for getting at what they believed were the basic teachings, valid for all. Contemporary Biblical scholarship shows the extent of efforts to discern various layers of discourse in the gospels, ranging from a handful of adamantine sayings of Jesus, which were embellished by his first disciples and expanded by first- and second-century scribes into the Four Gospels.

The Jesuit mission of bringing Christianity to the nooks and crannies of the world required even more emphasis on distinguishing essential dogmas from cultural variables. In that spirit, Jesuits had been initiated as Mandarins, Brahmins, Buddhist priests and Sufis, seeing no conflict between those spiritual roles and their dogmatic commitments. (Franciscan and Dominican theologians disagreed and eventually had the Jesuits outlawed for over a generation because of these practices.) Throughout my Jesuit education, I regularly read works by Asian, Middle Eastern and African (male) scholars and attended their lectures. Pedro Arrupe, appointed by Pope Paul VI as General towards the end of my Jesuit career, had been a Zen practitioner for twenty-five years before his appointment; *Time* ran a photo of him seated in the lotus posture.

Even though I was raised with that sense of cultural diversity, I was simultaneously taught that I was part of a community that had access to a transcultural grasp of reality. Christian theology, perennial philosophy and Western science gave us access, it was believed, to the nude body of Truth underneath its colorful ethnic dresses. It was not until I was directly engaged in the practice of Rolfing that I discovered my place within, not outside of culture.

SOME DAYS AFTER an excruciatingly painful second session of Rolfing with Ed Maupin, in which he spent the better part of an hour digging into the soles of my feet with his knuckles, I was doing my daily run through New Haven's Edgewood Park. I suddenly noticed that I was running on the balls of my feet, never letting my full sole touch the ground. Until that moment, it had seemed perfectly natural to run that way. As I continued to lope along, memories of my foot history flashed by. Because I had warts and severe ingrown toenails as a youngster, I would have to go around for months at a time in a shoe with a hole cut out, my infected big toe wrapped in a bandage. The podiatrist ascribed my problems to going barefoot, exposing myself to what he called the filth of beaches and public swimming pools. His warnings prompted me to develop the habit of walking on tiptoe to avoid the dreaded germs, a habit which oozed over into other activities like running. When I haltingly tried what it was like to run with the entire sole of my foot in contact with the ground, I first became aware of an intense fear that the weight of my body would crush the bones of my foot. I slowly accustomed myself to the fact that my bones were indeed strong enough to support me. A new and strangely delicious sensation came from that feeling of intimacy with the ground.

No sooner had I indulged in a few strides of that pleasurable contact than a raw fear quivered through me, like the night terrors that had often awakened me during childhood. It felt like I was jeopardizing myself by yielding to dangerous currents of energy "down below," which were beyond my control. Assuring myself that I was safe by attending to the sun coming through the young willow buds and the laughter of children in the playground, I forced myself to keep running with my feet on the ground, flooded with memories of teachings about purgatory, hell, Satan and his minions, sex and excrement. I realized that until then, I had never even questioned the assumption that linked spiritual excellence exclusively with the cultivation of only one of the many dimensions of the body—the upper pole of the vertical axis, while spiritual decadence was linked with the lower pole.

Jesus was said to have come *down* from heaven; dying, he *descended* into the realms of purgatory to gather the Old Testament saints, was raised from the dead and *ascended* back *up* into heaven. In a second great triumph over the power of death, the body of his mother Mary was taken *up* into heaven, the promise of our eventual ascensions.

According to the abstractions of Christian theology, spiritual evolution begins at inanimate rocks, progresses upward through plants, fish, birds and mammals until it reaches an immeasurable gulf bridged by God's creation of the soul breathed into mud to make human beings. Then the upward journey continues in the realm of this new soul-world, beginning with virtuous humans, continuing up into the heaven of humans who have died in sanctity, still higher into the multiple ranks of angels, archangels, thrones and dominions, seraphim and cherubim, reaching the pinnacle of spiritual evolution with the Blessed Virgin in front of the throne of the Holy Trinity. In mirror fashion, spiritual degradation descends below the middle-realm of soulless matter through the purgatorial realms of modest human vices until it reaches the Stygian barrier of no return, where again it descends through the seven realms of the deadly sinners into the lowest region of fallen saints and angels, to the nadir where the highest angel, Lucifer, the light-bearer, fell in his pride.

The value of a particular class of experiences is measured according to its location on that vertical axis. The scale of embodiment reflects that vertical system of values. The middle realm is that of guts breaking up foods to make flesh, gas, fat and excrement. Vulgar and disgusting, it is barely human. Both virtue and sin, of course, can occur in this realm. The good person is hygienic, regulated, has sex only with wife or husband, with genitals in their "natural" orifices, eats the proper foods and not excrement. Such virtues are hardly worth speaking of among Christians, a bare minimum for salvation. And their companion vices are modest, at their most extreme worthy only of a pass to the upper balconies of hell, populated by Boschian sodomites and adulterers. Saintly good and diabolic evil occur only in the person who stands upright like the old man's staff, either in prideful defiance of his Lord God and suppression of his fellows, or in the saintly offering of his intricate brain and elegant posture to the authority of Bible or Pope.

If asked, any theologian would say that "up" was only metaphorical; heaven and hell were in a different dimension than ours. But the barrage of Christian art, architecture and ritual prescriptions taught otherwise, imperceptibly habituating the believer to stretch up ever higher in his or her spiritual quest. Catholic and High Protestant liturgy are monodirectional, the priests and ministers entering at ground level processing upward towards the level of the church, ideally situated on a prominent rise, and even further upwards into pulpit and high altar. The movement patterns in those liturgies are straight-lined, priests, ministers and acolytes carrying themselves erect. Bows and prostrations are acknowledgments of "higher-ups." The great achievements of sacred architecture, whether Romanesque, Byzantine or Gothic, coax the eye upward, and hopefully the soul.

Monastic orders like the Jesuits give more explicit and refined attention to upward verticality in practices of kneeling, sitting upright and standing in meditation. Ignatius Loyola's "Rules of Modesty" reflected the widely held assumption that postural verticality served to spiritualize everyday activities of sitting at one's desk or walking down the hallway; in that spirit, the Rules proscribed rotational sashayings and swaggerings, slouchings and major *Arsenii*.

Ida Rolf was even more explicit about the spiritual significance of the upward, pinning it down to the proper cant of the cranium on the neck. As my experience of learning to run on the soles of my feet bears witness, she did indeed devote more attention than many students of the body to downward verticality, having developed an elaborate set of manipulations for the pelvis, legs, feet and ankles. Working with her over a decade taught me to inhabit my previously vacated nether regions. Her manipulations made me capable of overcoming fears of exploring the delights of the pelvis by learning how to allow genital sensations to radiate out through the hips, down the legs, up into the torso, producing orgasms that were as heavenly as our high school catechism promised. But that disciplined attention to the lower was always in service of enhancing the upward movement through the top of the head, where she located spiritual evolution: "This is what Rolfers are doing: we are lifting a body up. We're getting the uppermost pole of the body lifted up.... It all sounds so much alike: I will lift up my head; I am lifting toward the Lord; I am lifting toward the mountain. All religious thinking has tended to understand that there was a lifting up in terms of growth in the spiritual realm."[30] After all, baboons and elephants are well-grounded.

The West's exaltation of the vertical appears in its most abstract form in a long and continuous philosophical tradition, popularly called "the perennial philosophy," beginning with Plato and Aristotle, continuing up to the present day principally among esoteric thinkers, such as Fritjof Schuon, a member of the Sufi Order in the West:

> ...whereas the animal is horizontal and only advances toward itself—that is, it is enclosed within its own form—man, in advancing, transcends himself; even his forward movement seems vertical, it denotes a pilgrimage toward his Archetype, towards the celestial Kingdom, towards God. The beauty of the anterior side of the human body indicates the nobleness, on the one hand of man's vocational end, and on the other hand of his manner of approaching it; it indicates that man directs himself towards God and that he does so in a manner that is 'humanly divine,' if one may say so. But the posterior side of the body also has its meaning: it indicates, on the one hand the noble innocence of the origin, and on the other hand the noble manner of leaving behind himself what has been transcended; it expresses, positively, whence we have come and, negatively, how we turn our backs to what is no longer ourselves. Man comes from God and he goes towards God; but at the same time, he draws away from an imperfection which is no longer his own and draws nearer to a perfection which is not yet his.[31]

(It is hard to resist the temptation to create mental cartoons of that noble anterior with nose, penis and belly leading upwards towards his vocational end followed by his humble posterior!)

☙

AFTER COMPLETING MY Rolfing training in Big Sur and Pigeon Key, Florida, I moved with my new family of Elissa, Mike, Mora, and Rina from New Haven to Santa Fe, New Mexico, to set up our practice as Somatics therapists and to practice a life closer to nature, hiking in the mountains and cultivating a large garden on our fourteen-acre piece of land, with a century-old adobe house, four miles from the nearest paved road.

Living among the remains of the two-thousand-year-old Anasazi culture, and its heirs in the Tewa Pueblos of the Rio Grande, I was jarred to discover that this ancient tradition emphasized the spiritual aspects of the lower pole. Its most obvious manifestation was in sacred architecture. While Christian churches are ideally placed on hills, with tall spires, raised altars and interiors designed to uplift, here the ceremonial gathering place was the kiva. Not only was it below ground level, entered by climbing down a ladder, but the most sacred space within it was yet a lower and smaller hole, the *sipapu*, the gateway to and from the realms of the gods who dwelt not only on mountain summits, sky and stars, but within the belly of the earth.

The Pueblo rituals involve a circulation of downward movement into the kiva, still lower through the *sipapu* into the depths of the earth, and upward movements out into the plazas of the pueblos and further up the holy streams into the sacred mountains. The specific pattern of body movement in these rituals embodies the sacred quality of the downward. In contrast to the ever upward-striving aesthetic of Christian-inspired European ballet, the Pueblo dancers drive their feet heavily downward in response to the sonorous and repetitive beating of the drums. The ground itself becomes a resonant drum, throbbing with the percussion of hundreds of feet. The movement is not exclusively downward; the torso and head remain erect. Like Chinese t'ai chi chu'an and qi gong, the movement patterns honor both poles of the vertical.

But even more challenging to my monotheistic metaphysics was the realization that up-down vertical was only one of many directions honored in their theology. Dance, ritual movements, the design of costumes and the location of homes and kivas within the pueblos honor a multiplicity of compass directions, including vectors towards the sacred mountains, rivers and the annual course of sun, moon and stars. A traditional healer from the Vancouver region writes of his people's poly-directional choreography:

> Dancing is both a spiritual and a physical prayer. For instance, our stomp dance helps us get the life force flowing. When we stomp our feet in time with the drum, we are connecting our spiritual roots with Mother Earth's roots, her veins. At the same time that we're stomping our feet, our hands are dancing. They're reaching for medicine; they're reaching for healing and strength. Another dance, the spin dance, helps us untie and regenerate ourselves. We get dizzy from spinning, but afterwards we see things differently.[32]

In addition to sacred architecture, I encountered in the pueblos another challenge to my heavenward oriented spirituality: sitting cross-legged on the ground.

I had already gotten an introduction to the spiritual significance of cross-legged sitting at Gia Fu Feng's Santa Cruz mountain retreat center. In my final years of theology, I had devoted some time to the study of Buddhism and Hinduism and had learned of the spiritual significance embodied in images of the sitting Buddha. But I was still heavily influenced by Christian and Rolf verticalism, which viewed such practices as less evolved. Moreover, until I lived in New Mexico, I assumed that when native peoples sat on the ground it was not like the aesthetic practice of *zazen*, but because they were more primitive, lacking the niceties of ordinary furniture and European manners. It soon became clear that sitting in the sweat circle, meeting lodge or alone in the wilderness during fasts had evolved as a spiritual practice for cultivating an intimacy with the earth and a more egalitarian feeling for each other. I puzzled that such sitting did not produce among the Pueblo dwellers the kind of collapse that Western theorists said it would; their torsos and heads were unusually erect, not caved in like mine and so many of my Caucasian clients. They also seemed to have qualities that are rare in the Anglo world: a coyote irony, a mud-head lack of pretentiousness, a corn-mother easiness with human foibles.

Cross-legged sitting seemed to carry a sense of values that could not be expressed solely in the vertical.

❀

I DO NOT mean to enshrine the cross-legged sitting posture. As those of us with back problems know, it is more difficult to get up from that posture. We know the relief of sitting in a chair in contrast with having to sit for long periods without support on the floor or ground. What is at issue here is the exclusive identification of any particular posture or direction with the spiritual. The point is to have a multi-directional spirituality.

The Tewa, for example, sacralize directionality not as irrevocably linked to evolution or degradation but as indicating different spiritual challenges. Virtue and vice on the multi-directional medicine wheel are not identified with one direction rather than another. They invoke the uniquely different challenges associated with different directions. The Parsifalian journey upwards is indeed well covered by Christian theology. But the journey downwards has its own characteristics, symbolized by coping with fears of snakes, fiery lava and the dark. Journeys to the North involve learning how to survive in extremes of temperature variation, keeping oneself warm in the ice, snow and raging winds. Dealing with the South requires one to learn to live with the relentless glare of the sun, the always verdant vegetation with its fierce insects and reptiles, the dank air. Looking to the East, one is faced with the challenges of wakefulness, the beginnings of illumination; to the West, with the inception of darkness, the monsters of the night, the end.

The native elders, as much as Christians, are concerned about human values — love, compassion, truth-telling, honoring relatives, caring for the needy. They do not, however, associate these virtues exclusively with uprightness, but also with downwardness, frontwardness, backwardness, sidewardness and round-aboutness.

In my encounters with the Rio Grande culture, I began to get a sense that the institutions which shaped me were trying to reach too high too fast, neglecting the more basic realities of trees, animals, clear water and air. I became aware of a weariness deep in my bones caused by an over-reaching, a world-weariness which I could see in other Western idealists, Christian, Marxist, Freudian and Positivist, always rushing somewhere else in a hurry to change the way things are, convinced that we possess the unique path to Truth, failing in that Promethean rush to see the beauty at hand, with its alternative truths. Attending the seasonal rituals in the pueblos and hiking with Elissa among Anasazi ruins in the canyons of the Pajarito plateau were eroding my destiny-freighted viewpoint that I belonged to a special community in possession of the true story into which other stories had to be translated.

IN 1976, BY STRANGE coincidence I had as clients two women who were about the same age and had remarkably similar body-structures. One was Hopi, whom I will call "Iris"; the other, Japanese-American, "Rowena." They both complained of extreme back pain, Iris in her lower back, Rowena in her upper back and neck. Yet they both had spinal columns which appeared to be nearly perfectly straight. That straightness puzzled me.

Ida Rolf, like many specialists in the area of body structure, had argued that our evolution from primates leaves us—that is, *all* human beings—in an awkward state on the way towards the upright posture at which we have not yet arrived. According to her and many other experts in body structure, a major symptom of that unfinished evolution is a frontward curvature, "lordosis," of the vertebrae of the lower back and neck. A well-known specialist in physical medicine goes so far as to call these two lordotic curvatures, "man's antigravity destiny."[33]

The manipulative techniques of Rolfing, which by then I had practiced for five years, were designed to lengthen the tissues surrounding those vertebrae with the goal of freeing the spinal column to right itself towards the imaginary plumb line of the Rolf Template. (Despite subtle technical arguments about the precise shapes of the ideal spinal contours, people like F. M. Alexander, Moshe Feldenkrais and Françoise Mézieres, including the schools of chiropractic and osteopathy, structured their body manipulations around similar goals.)

But after several sessions with Iris and Rowena within the Rolf context, I could no longer avoid the fact that their spinal columns did not have the destined antigravity curves; theirs were virtually straight. I felt like I had reached to open a door and, because the knob slipped off into my hand as I stepped forward to walk through it, I bumped right into it. I was in darkness, not comprehending what I saw and felt in their necks and lower backs.

Until I encountered these two women, there had been a relatively easy relationship between my ideas of the body and the feelings in my hands on another person. The way that I organized my touching people from session to session had produced generally good results, and I had some confidence that I knew what I was doing. I had taken for granted that everyone's spinal column more or less followed a relatively standard pattern of deviation from the normal, based on the assumption that as human beings we were all at the same stage of biological evolution. I also took for granted that differences of perception and worldview followed a similar pattern of deviation from a set of universal truths valid for all. I had, of course, always known that other people were different from me, often radically so. But I had always assumed that those differences were essentially superficial: although a person standing on a mountain sees things differently from a person in a swamp, the same kind of looker, with the same fundamental structures, peers out of those two different locations. At a deep level, all humans saw things the same way, if they were honest according to the norms of Western psychology and their body structures were on the way towards the Rolf Line.

It took an intimate meeting with two people from ancient cultures different from my own to make me realize that I could not inhabit anyone else's viewpoint. Here I *knew* that I could not see and feel things the way they did. But not because of anything they said or any peculiar feelings they expressed: in idiom, expression of emotions and life-style, they were as thoroughly Americanized as I or any of my other clients. Outside of those sessions, it would never have occurred to me that Iris and Rowena were so foreign to my sensibilities. My humbling sense of their otherness came exclusively from the rupture between my sensations of them and the Rolf ideas guiding my hands-on work.

In that conceptual blackout, I was forced to turn to something more primal than the Template and Recipe. I was left with bare intuition and simple sensations of my hand touching them with more inquisitiveness than before. I had to pay more attention to the subtle responses of their flesh to my touch and give more weight to their verbal feedback, having to reach out to them more than usual, asking them questions about their responses, about who they were.

In the case of the Rowena, the results of our work over a period of three months were very modest, her neck pain abating somewhat but not enough to excite her about our work. She was a computer programmer in a local electronics firm. Our relationship was flat; we didn't have much to say to each other except about matters directly related to the work of Rolfing, and I was unable to make much headway in finding how to contact her bodily tissues or her personality in a meaningful way. I eventually lost touch with her.

Things were different with Iris. Like myself, she was stumbling her way along a rocky spiritual path. She had been so frightened as a child by the spiritual powers of her grandparents, that she had renounced the old ways and opted for the life of a secular artist. But in recent years, she was finding her way back to her culture and was now engaged in reviving the traditional Hopi methods of weaving and pottery. Our interactions produced the sparks of friendship. We shared an easy humor, enjoyed talking about films, novels, our writing and our similar attempts to find a more grounded spiritual practice. In that context of personal connection, I was able to find subtle ways of using my hands to evoke movement from the tissues deep within her bodily structure. She experienced significant relief of her back pain from our sessions and returned periodically for work over a number of years. I eventually officiated at her wedding to a young poet on the Tsankawi Plateau above the Rio Grande.

Strangely enough, after my conceptually clear ways of proceeding were disrupted by not knowing what to do next, I felt more like Ida, who never seemed to be occupied by external ideals, but was rather deeply in touch with the uniqueness of the bodily tissues of the person with whom she was working. For her and for other effective Rolfers with whom I have worked over the years, the Template functioned more as a background theme, with the felt sense of the individual in the foreground. I had been so immersed in the world of concepts that the Template captivated an inordinate amount of my attention. Being forced to find some other way of relating to these two women helped me along the pilgrimage out of the brittle world of theories into the immediacy of flesh and emotion.

In the attempt to make sense of what I was feeling and seeing in Rowena and Iris, a glimmer of light came from noticing that their physical structures were not completely unfamiliar. Although they did not look like what Euro-American physical experts said all spines looked like at this point in evolution, they did remind me of other forms I had seen. Iris mirrored what I had often seen among inhabitants of the pueblos. Her physique had the unusual combination both of solidity and grace that I had been noticing when I was walking the narrow streets of Walpi or Shungopavi, taking part in the bean dances, watching the kachinas emerge from the kivas with the snow-capped San Francisco peaks in the background. Rowena reminded me of images I had seen in Asian art, dance and meditation postures.

From my earlier studies of Renaissance philosophy, I was familiar with the perception of the human body as the microcosmic reflection of the cosmos, an image which I took to be biological and soulful: the cellular intricacies of the body contained all of the intricacies that one could find in the universe; the soul, by virtue of its capacities to question and love, was a representation of the spiritual vastness of reality. But here I was confronted with the macro-culture in the micro-culture. My contact with each of these women was not simply a matter of one person touching another with certain therapeutic goals in mind, nor just the interaction between two people complicated by the psychodynamics of unique family histories, one male and the other female, with all of those complications. It was an encounter between two different embodiments of ancient rituals, culturally sanctioned postures and movement patterns, cuisine, attitudes towards sexuality, disease, birth and death.

At this our *fin de siècle,* we know a lot about the dangers inherent in such meetings. On the one hand, there are the outbursts of creativity which one finds in the coming together of artists, scientists, athletes, spiritual teachers and community organizers from different cultures. But there are also the many forms of colonization where the practices of one culture are subsumed by another, co-opted, brutalized, even eliminated.

My reflections on my work with Iris and Rowena made me painfully aware that I had deceived myself in thinking that I had left behind missionary zeal when I put aside my Jesuit soutane. I was confronted by the humbling realization that the colonial mentality existed deeper within my neuropeptides. I was still engaged in an attempt to convert people to a particular view of the world. I had now adopted the peculiar, but no less effective means of manipulating their flesh and bones in the direction of the Template to produce the kind of consciousness defined by Ida Rolf. Instead of using my skills to help my clients find their unique ways to respond to the challenges offered by their own histories to liberate and enrich their own points of view, I was attempting to mold them into someone else's notions about experience.

I had taken the Rolf Line for the privileged path to Truth, applicable to all people, when, in fact, it is an unusually useful symbol created by an upper middle-class Long Island woman, inspired by some sixty years of successful healing work almost exclusively with upper-class white people in the United States and Great Britain. It has neither more nor less relation to absolute truth than many other ideals: here, the ancient Japanese and Hopi ideals embodied in their different expressions of art, ritual dance, meditation practices, methods of healing, martial arts and kachinas.

As I attempted to extricate myself from the confusions provoked by trying to alleviate the pain of Iris and Rowena, I came across the work of a small group of scholars who have organized their research around a brief 1933 essay of Marcel Mauss, *"Les techniques du corps."* By "techniques of the body," Mauss meant the wide range of activities which shape the protean body of the infant into an adult, ranging from styles of caring for infants, to gender formation, styles of work, exercise, sexual postures, dance and ritual. He argued that these activities, which seem so "natural" are actually highly articulated expressions of a particular culture's values; if you examine any particular technique such as using a shovel, you will find that the technique, and the body it goes towards shaping, differ from culture to culture. During the past sixty years, that thesis has been substantiated by a number of anthropological researchers.[34]

Those events initiated me into what has now been a twenty-year study of the variety of ways in which different cultures organize their values and how those values are expressed in bodily practices. They also took some of the pressure off my back. Since high school gym classes, I had been attempting to force my sore spinal column into an ill-fitting ideal shape. I began to explore more internal clues about directions for movement suggested by my sensations and created for myself a discipline of idiosyncratic stretches, bends and aerobic movements. As I allowed myself to be more who I was in the very physical sense of being stiff and relatively immobile in my spinal structures, a new relief began to emerge, along with curious new ranges of subtle movement.

With my clients, I let myself be drawn away from the overwhelming domination of abstract ideas about body structure into primal senses of body movement, the feel of my palm on another's skin, and the impact of another's voice, leaving me with a more intimate emotional contact with other persons and the world. As my path veered in that direction, I was struck by its profound capacities for healing the divisions that haunt our personal relationships and our social world; it was a path of common sense, uncluttered with the jabber of centuries.

In light of those kinds of experiences my eventual discovery of Emilie Conrad Da'Oud felt like bumping into a long-lost friend deep in backcountry wilderness. I am going to give some of the details of her life and the evolution of her work as a way of showing how these multicultural ideas about the body might be applied.

E~MILIE CREATED HER~ Somatics method, Continuum, when she, like myself, found herself having to work her way out of a squeeze between two cultures. Born and raised in Brooklyn during the 1930s and 1940s, she says that she was driven as an adolescent to look for something more primal than she found in everyday life. At first she imagined that she could find it in primitive dance, and began studying with its leading teachers, Katherine Dunham, Pearl Primus and Sevilla Fort. She went to Haiti in 1955 where she spent five years studying Haitian dance and religion, even starting her own dance troupe there. A dark Sephardic Jew, she became even darker, braiding her hair and taking on the character of the Island women to such an extent that Eastman-Kodak photographers on a search for "beauties of the Caribbean" photographed her. When she returned to New York in 1960, she was confronted with that photograph mounted on the Grand Central billboard over the title "La Belle Creole." She realized that something drastic had happened to her in between the two cultures; she has described it to me as entering a long-term existential breakdown related to "the dissonance between the liquid, organic rhythms of Haiti and the frantic, manufactured pace of Manhattan."

Without her realizing it, her physical appearance had become so altered that she looked like a Haitian and was unable to get the kinds of jobs that had been readily available to her before she left New York. She had to turn to professional modeling and the teaching of primitive dance. On occasion, she and her troupe did performances in nightclubs based on voodoo rituals. She has recounted to me a night during an ecstatic solo fire dance, when she suddenly felt she had "crossed over, beyond the possibility of ever coming back." That "crossing over" meant for her the breakdown of her culture, with all of the categories of meaning and bodily expression. The dissolution was so far reaching that it would take her some years to create a replacement. In the meantime, she had to put up with an uncomfortable, sometimes almost psychotic sense of disorientation, which she now attributes to the fact that she was strongly resisting the implications of that deeper sense of her body for the outlines of a new view of reality. Her link to reality became a series of events in which she found herself returning with increasing clarity into a primal area of experience.

In this disoriented condition, she entered into a new marriage in 1963 and moved to Los Angeles. In 1964, just learning to drive for the first time, she lost control of her VW bug convertible on the Santa Ana Freeway and collided with a semi. In the instant before collision, at which point her VW was totally destroyed, her entire life flashed in front of her. She felt a hand come down over her and say "No!" She emerged from the wreckage without a scratch, with the feeling that the "no" was a warning that it was dangerous for her to continue fighting so hard to hold away what she had learned from the cultural crossover.

Then in 1967, she finally went all the way into what she calls her "black hole." She describes herself as "falling completely apart," unable to get out of bed to go to her job as a model. She continually felt dizzy and was besieged by voices and visions. When she shut her eyes, a characteristic feeling came upon her, followed by the appearance of a "screen" before her eyes, on which she saw with great clarity detailed scenes of ancient cultures. At the same time, her body began to move in certain ways which she recognized as what she was looking for when twenty years before she had set about studying primitive dance. It was her good luck to have been in therapy with a psychiatrist who did not view her experience as pathological but recognized it as an interim condition between systems of meaning, one of which has lost its sense, the other of which is just beginning to form. Confident that she was bringing something forth, he encouraged her to go into her visions and try to make sense of them.

She describes her crisis as falling into a crack between two cultures and finding her own body underneath the cultural forms of each. "I had to give up everything I believed. I saw that what I called 'my body'—how I moved, talked, even how I thought—was a cultural imprint. With all my training, I had been teaching 'my body' to dance. But deep inside there was already a dance going on, if I would perceive it—a dance of myriad movement forms beyond anything I could think of. I had to feel it. I had to let it guide me."[35]

I want to underscore the commonplace illusion that took so long for Emilie to unravel. It is the notion that "New York" represents a complex, highly-evolved cultural form while primitive dance is "natural." (For Emilie and other Somatics theorists, "natural" meant "better," while for other people, it means "of less value." Neither view is accurate.) Lying in her bed, moving to her visions and voices, she realized that both New York and Haiti are equally sophisticated cultural forms, each shaping the raw materials of life. Her long sought-after "primitive" had always existed in movements which are occurring in us willy-nilly: cellular, respiratory, circulatory, peristaltic, nervous, lymphatic, micro-muscular.

As with other Somatics innovators like Alexander, Feldenkrais, and Bonnie Bainbridge Cohen, it took Emilie several years to distill those experiences into a definitive method. The first stage was in response to people who asked her to teach primitive dance, which she used as a vehicle for teaching those more basic kinds of movements. A second crucial stage was her puzzling about the nature of paralysis. If the very essence of material reality is movement, what does it mean when a person has a pathology that manifests itself in immobility?

With that question in mind, she began working with people with severe neuromuscular disorders and from them learned more clearly what was involved in her own experiences. She worked with a twenty-three-year-old woman, Susan, who had been partially paralyzed by polio since age one. She had always been told by physicians that she would never recover movement in her left leg, because current medical belief assumes that polio causes muscles and nerves to degenerate in such a way that the paralysis is irreversible. Working without any familiar concepts of spinal alignment to guide her, as I had been forced to do with Iris and Rowena, Emilie simply stayed present with her hands on the young woman's body. She sat like this for hours at a stretch, giving no instructions, not even guiding her in visualizations. At first, Susan felt only heat. Then one day the leg began to shudder and move in strange ways that were similar to the ways that Emilie had found herself moving in her bed. Over a four-year period of weekly four-hour sessions, many of which were observed and subjected to electromyographical analysis in the UCLA kinesiology laboratory, Susan manifested a range of subtle and finely articulated movements. Emilie's experience with Susan and similar cases led her to recognize the healing capacities in movements that are not ordinarily attended to in the public world, in fact movements that a culture may not even recognize *as* movements. "Paralyzed people," she writes, "can feel movement inside their bodies, but because our culture does not value this kind of movement, they think they cannot move. Helping Susan get in touch with the movement within her atrophied leg allowed the inner movement to surface and ripple across the skin and eventually enabled Susan to lift her leg."[36]

One of my graduates, Irene Lober, eventually published her master's thesis on how she came to discover these same kinds of movements trying to heal herself after she incurred a spinal cord injury and paraplegia after an automobile accident near her home in Germany.[37] She now walks again, dances, hikes and skis, after having been told by physicians that she would never be able to use her legs again.

Another clue came to Emilie from her inner voices, one saying to her: "Your movement is too muscular; sound will lead you into a more refined level of movement." She realized how easy it is for a person who deliberately undertakes movement—exercise, dance, sports, even "Sensory Awareness"—to adopt a familiar muscular pattern. She began to use sound to find something else. She would deliberately create unfamiliar sounds such as those resulting from directing sounds far back in the throat or vibrating the tongue against the palate. She would sit quietly observing the kinds of movements that would be generated throughout the interior of the body, allowing those movements to reverberate, sometimes to the point of moving her body in space.

On the basis of those experiences, her work evolved from teaching primitive dance and working as a hands-on healer to a radically simplified form in which she now helps large groups of people locate unfamiliar movements, and explore how those movements might expand into life. She might have a group spend several hours initiating the tiniest movements of a finger or knee, and then exploring the ripples of subtle reactions put into action by those micromovements. Or she might suggest spending hours, even days, making tiny, virtually inaudible sounds and observing their effects throughout the interior regions of the body.

After a lifetime with a stiff spine, it was a delicious experience to encounter this work. The Somatics world, with its constant focus on body structure, had made me painfully aware of the limitations of my spinal movement and deeply envious of those sensuous and athletic spinal torsions, backward and forward curves of which I was incapable. Fellow therapists in their zeal for evolved physical structures would approach me with patronizing concern, offering unsolicited interpretations and cures for my stiffness. But here in these classes, I discovered infinite possibilities of movement in my spinal column. I found myself able to descend for hours at a time into the experience of the slightest movement of my vertebrae, finding there unnameable sensible and sensuous pleasures. And I began to feel better about myself, appreciating a subtlety and grace, in both movement and thought, that were uniquely mine.

I also found myself in altered states of consciousness which yielded a different sense of the transcendent than I had experienced in meditation or in using psychedelics. Like Rolfing, the experiences of Continuum are radically sensual; they are not visualizations, images or ideas. They seduce one's attention from the chatter of inner conversations and the barrage of colorful images, as Buddhist meditation does, deep into the immediacy of a specific movement—the "nowhere" of Ignatius Loyola. At the same time, the consciousness provoked by that sensual attention has the qualities that mystics have traditionally identified with the spiritual: the dissolution of experienced barriers between self and other, body and mind, self and physical world.

While I had found that many anthropologists and sociologists had studied the embodiment of culture, Emilie was the first whose actual method of Somatics reflected those ideas. Hers is a deconstructive work that allows one to probe into the more basic movements that have given rise to a particular cultural form. Different spiritual traditions have put their attention on one or a few primal movements—sitting, breathing, sensing. Over time, sometimes centuries, they develop their rituals and meditation practices by collective repetition and refinement of that family of movements. The resultant experiences produce their culturally unique somato-spiritual practices: zazen, hatha yoga, t'ai chi chu'an, sufi whirling, the hesychastic breathing of Russian Orthodox mystics. As the practices grow older and become more formalized, their roots in the more basic spontaneous movements are forgotten. Continuum, not unlike Edmund Husserl's eidetic phenomenology, teaches a person how to investigate any particular form, ranging from meditation postures to forms of calisthenics, and find one's way into the primal movements that have become somatically conceptualized in that particular way.

The spirit arises at the moment of contact with the primal, at that very moment when we step into territories that do not appear on familiar maps. Insistence on sticking to the maps leads one to overlook the primal and bypass the realm of spirit. As long as I clung to my abstract ideas about body structure, I failed to touch the reality of the Hopi and the Japanese-American women; when I allowed myself to fall into blankness, I felt and saw them intimately. While Emilie fought to continue defining herself as a New York Jew or as a teacher of Creole dance, she descended further into confusion; when she finally allowed herself to move in unfamiliar ways, she stumbled upon the primal reality for which she had searched since childhood.

An impossible separation between "nature" and "culture" is not the issue here. The words that have seemed apt both for my own experiences and for Emilie's are functional ones like "basic," "simple," "primal." When I lost a sense of what to do in my work with Iris and Rowena, I had to turn to simpler forms of touching, seeing and listening. In the depths of what she calls the "black hole" of her existential breakdown, Emilie let herself move in even more idiosyncratic ways than she had learned in "primitive" dance, using movements that do not appear on the maps of Western medical kinesiology.

THE RAPID PROLIFERATION of inter-cultural knowledge at this moment in history has evoked a number of responses. One is to try for a homogenization of human beings, reducing them to the lowest common denominators: Levi's jeans, McDonald's, Madonna. Another is to retreat in fear into enclaves of one's own kind: churches, walled suburbs and rococo theologies. Still another is to junk one's own culture and adopt the costumery of another. None of these moves are promising for healing the ragged tears in our social fabric; they are, rather, movements of despair.

A turn to more primal realities could lay the groundwork for methods of joining with people of many cultures and ideologies in journeys of investigation into how we might deal with common problems of hunger, disease, broken relationships and a poisoned environment. And how we might celebrate our shared delight in clear air and water, in touching and being touched with affection, in care for one another.

Scarred Bodies, Broken Hearts

MEETINGS BETWEEN CULTURES involve more than personal, individual mistakes. The history of those meetings is a story of continuous attempts of one group to snuff out the spirits of another by publicly sanctioned abuse of flesh.

I began to learn that sad history in my infancy when I sensed the bitterness borne by my Irish-born relatives towards the British Anglican nobility who had driven them off their farmland. Growing up in a city where Roman Catholics were a small minority, I had a sense that our faith put us at odds with the political establishment. My catechism teachers said that our beliefs about the sacredness of the individual body and the outpouring of the Holy Spirit into the hearts of every person were such a threat to Jewish and Roman authorities that they led to Jesus' crucifixion. Throughout Asia Minor and the Roman Empire, Christians had been put to death because those beliefs led them to defy the patriarchal and slave-holding social order.

I was schooled within a militant anti-Communist climate, which was the most recent of repeated conflicts between secular authority and Christian ideas. Shortly after World War II, a wave of European immigrant priests gave sermons at the Sacramento Cathedral about how Russian Communists had used torture and drugs to make them renounce their religious beliefs. They knew that the way to alter the spirit was through maiming the flesh. The Church was inundated with a wave of conversions to Roman Catholicism of European Communists, many of whom wrote lurid accounts of how the Party viewed Rome as its most serious threat. The teachings supposedly given by the Blessed Virgin at Fatima in Portugal in 1917 to three young school children had become a popular cult. In those visions, Mary proclaimed a cosmic battle between Rome and Moscow; the victory, she said, would go to Christians only if they engaged more seriously in prayer and physical penance.

Mao Tse Tung's persecutions brought these ideas closer to home. Many California priests had gone to China as missionaries. They were imprisoned during the revolution and tortured in the most brutal ways. Throughout high school, college and my years in the Jesuits, I had regular contact with men who had been left enfeebled and even permanently crippled by months, sometimes years, of torture and brainwashing techniques in Chinese prisons. The point of the elaborate torture techniques was not simply to destroy the person; killing would more efficiently accomplish that. Like their Christian predecessors in the Roman and Spanish Inquisitions who tortured Jews, Muslims, "pagans" and Christian mystics, the Communists wanted a public renunciation of what they viewed as heretical beliefs. In a particularly tragic case, a young Jesuit whom I knew succumbed after six months' confinement in a four-foot cubed cell wired with amplified voices twenty-four hours a day. He signed a document renouncing his faith and returned to California humiliated.

Studies of theology often centered on the interaction between Christian beliefs about *body* and *spirit*, and secular notions of authority. Southern Ireland, Franco Spain and post-war Italy were models of the traditional Vatican policy. The official belief was that the body is sacred and immortal, thus the State had the holy task of regulating those activities which would impinge on that sacredness: sexual intercourse, marriage and divorce, abortion, birth control, and pornography. The official Roman teaching then as now is that such matters should not be left to politicians who do not share Christian beliefs. Rome had condemned liberal thinkers like Jesuits Karl Rahner and John Courteney Murray for arguing that true spirituality flourished better when it was kept apart from political systems. When John Kennedy came upon the scene, he had to cite the teachings of such maverick theologians in response to widespread and well-grounded fears of papal interference in American politics.

I was always aware of the overwhelming presence of torture and war in human life. I remember seeing the early newsreels of the Holocaust taken when the liberation armies first came to the camps. My classical education in Xenophon, Thucydides, Julius Caesar and Toynbee made me intellectually familiar with how the maiming of flesh has been a major human occupation. I was haunted by film and television images of nuclear explosions. I had been sufficiently affected by images of the Vietnam war that I had turned in my draft card and joined the Resistance, an organization under the leadership of William Sloane Coffin. I knew that my Hopi client belonged to those generations of native Americans who had been displaced from their lands and often slaughtered, although it is only recently that I learned that the number of victims surpassed the number of those killed in the Holocaust. I also knew that the Japanese-American woman had parents who had been interred at the Tule Lake concentration camp during World War II, even though their families had been in this country longer than many of my relatives. My father had actually supervised its construction.

And yet, from the vantage point of the European-based stories I will tell in this chapter, the contours of my California viewpoint showed as little effect of that history of violence as do the beaches of Malibu when compared to the beaches of Normandy and the Bay of Naples, with their ruins of pillboxes, castles and monuments to war heroes. Life in the quiet river town of Sacramento, and later along the redwood forests and beaches of the Pacific, was not conducive to making those realities penetrate my guts and neurons. There seemed to be an unspoken agreement among Sacramentans that the evils experienced by our families in the past, and now being visited upon countless other fellow humans in other parts of the world, including our own riverfront slums, would be better forgotten. Even when I left the Sacramento Valley haze for the politically turbulent coast, I found that it was hard to get a feel for the brokenness of the world that matched my knowledge of its history.

❀

ELISSA AND I saved up enough money to make a four-month trip to Europe in 1979, our first. We both felt that the idealistic passions which had originally brought us together a decade earlier were flagging as we settled into our homestead, raising our children and working, I as a Rolfer, she as an Aston-Patterner (a system of body movement re-education, once affiliated with the Rolf Institute). Our original dream when we trained to practice these new therapies was that we would travel lightly in life, going where it seemed that we could best follow our visionary notions. We had imagined traveling about the world with our work, but as yet we had rarely left the Southwest, and then only for California or New York.

A combination of unforeseen circumstances prompted us to live in Paris for over a year and travel throughout Europe. A friend offered us an inexpensive flat in Paris for the year that she would be studying in Canada. Mora and Mike were in college. Rina was between eighth grade and high school, and it would be a natural time for her to spend a year in a French lycée. Elissa was under contract with Simon and Schuster to write a book on issues confronting middle-aged women (eventually published in 1983 as *Mirror, Mirror: The Terror of Not Being Young*), and she was eager to have the chance to interview women in Europe as well as in the United States.

The crucial element—financial support—appeared in the form of an invitation for me to practice Rolfing in the Montparnasse studio of Thérèse Bertherat, a famous author and body therapist.

Thérèse had until recently been an upper middle-class Parisian socialite wife and mother of two who had been married to a psychiatrist. On the afternoon of her fortieth birthday, he was called to his hospital for an emergency with one of his patients. As he walked through the entrance, his patient appeared with a gun, shot and killed him. She wrote a touching description of how she went about rebuilding her life after that tragedy in her first book, *The Body (le corp) Has Its Reasons.* (The English translation does not do justice to the French, which puns on Pascal's "the heart *(le coeur)* has its reasons of which the mind is ignorant.") Healing her grief came about as she discovered the same primal path into the explorations of body sensations and movement that had drawn Emilie and myself. She was particularly taken by the work of two older Parisian women, Lilly Ehrenfried and Françoise Mézieres.

Dr. Lilly Ehrenfried, who had been a physician in Berlin in the 1920s and early 1930s, was one of the first pupils of Elsa Gindler, the founder of an unnamed work that Charlotte Selver would eventually call "Sensory Awareness." She had also studied F. M. Alexander's technique and was schooled in the extensive German research on the relations between bodily posture and function. On April 1st, 1933, after the burning of the Reichstag and the decree ordering the identification of Jewish passports, Ehrenfried was urged to leave Berlin by a colleague, himself a refugee from Russia where he had been Lenin's personal physician. She fled to Paris and then to the South of France where she remained in hiding during the Occupation. After the war, she returned to Paris and eventually began teaching the Gindler work and hatha yoga. She was still teaching when I was there, at ninety years old, active and supple.

Thérèse writes that practicing Ehrenfried's teachings on how to direct her attention towards primal sensations of standing, feeling her feet on the ground and breathing helped her return into her own skin, where she found a refuge from the despair of being cast adrift in grief over the sudden loss of her husband. But that subtle work was not enough to heal her wounds. She needed something deeper and more vigorous, which she eventually found in the work of Françoise Mézieres.

Mézieres had been a prominent professor in a training college for what the French call *"kinésithérapie,"* somewhat like our field of physical therapy. But she came to realize that the dominant model of that field was too mechanistic. Its practitioners relied heavily on the use of complicated machinery to manipulate people. Their theoretical language was dominated by the image of the person as a mechanically-ordered body. She resigned her post and became an outspoken critic of the field. She developed her own system of manipulation, not unlike Rolfing, in which the practitioner manipulates the body of the client with his or her own hands, shaping that client towards an explicitly defined body ideal. That ideal was even more ethnically biased than Ida's: the shape of the body as it appeared in fifth century B.C. Greek sculpture. The Mézieres work was so effective in bringing Thérèse out of her depression that she had become as zealous a missionary for that Greek image as I had been for Ida's. Thérèse writes:

> She taught us not to accept any treatment that is not directed toward that perfect form. The Greek artist didn't attempt to express psychological, mystical or political contradictions— but rather a corporal and moral unity toward which each mortal, out of self-respect, should direct himself. Any deviation from this description individuates a corporal deformity.[38]

Le corp a ses raisons struck a chord in the French public that earlier books on the body had not, including a marvelous book by Ehrenfried herself.[39] It became a best-seller and the French began to flock to Thérèse and other body therapists, most of whom had been trained in the United States. By the time I arrived in Paris, there were six thriving Esalen-like growth centers there, more than in San Francisco, Los Angeles or New York. Confronted with this new clientele and with little training or experience as a therapist, like myself after Rolfing school, Thérèse often became frustrated that the Mézieres strategies of manipulation were not bringing some of her clients into ideal alignment. Shortly before I arrived, she had met a visiting novice Rolfer whose physical vigor caught her notice, and she judged that it would be a useful adjunct to the Mézieres work for clients who required more force to shape them into the ideal body. Having read my first book, *The Protean Body*, she saw in me an opportunity to have that help and invited me to Rolf in her studio. Naively impressed by her elegant Montparnasse studio with its romantic location just behind Hemingway's favorite bar, *La Closerie des Lilas*, and by the opportunity to spend a year learning the language by working with French clients, I accepted her offer, against the advice of Elissa, who distrusted Thérèse's preoccupation with external bodily symmetry.

I suddenly found myself immersed in politically-abused flesh. In a typical day, I would see four or five clients with stories like these:

- Françoise was a middle-aged Belgian aristocrat, tiny and intense, married, with a young son. During the war, her parents used their chateau near Brussels to hide Jews fleeing from Hitler. When Françoise was four years old, the Gestapo arrived in the middle of the night and took away her parents, whom she never saw or heard of again. She and her three-year-old sister were left alone with the servants for over six months before relatives came to care for them. She was seeking help, she said, for her chronic feelings of bleakness about everything in life; she was helpless in feeling any affection towards her husband or her young son. Despite the fact that she was well-toned, wiry and athletic, her flesh felt opaque, almost wooden, to my touch.

- Abdul Shalan was an Egyptian Muslim, executive assistant to the Secretary General of UNESCO. As a young economics professor, he had been put in jail by Nasser for several years and subjected to severe torture. His legs bore scars left by chains; his back had old welts left by beatings. His overall body structure, however, was in unusually good alignment. But he complained of feelings of bleakness. He had a hard time sleeping. He was lonely, often in despair.

- The 6-foot 5-inch, heavy and muscular fifty-five-year-old Duc de Querçize's body was filled with shrapnel: you could see pockets of it bulging under the skin of his heavily muscled arms, abdomen and legs. With pride, he told me stories of how he had collected it over a period of years of military service in Indochina and Algeria, in the proud tradition of the men of his lineage. He said that those lumps were his version of the dueling scars that distinguished the proud faces of his male ancestors. He was a member of Archbishop LeFevre's traditionalist Catholic church, which held that the Vatican Council's reforms were heretical. When I asked him why he had come to me, he put his hand on his lumbar spine. Thérèse had told him that it had too much sway in it and that she was too small to manipulate it into its proper position. She told him that I could do that.

- Charles was a well-known *couturier* (clothes-maker), a lean, good-looking athletic man of fifty, married with two teenage daughters, Jewish. When he was eleven years old, the concierge in his family's Right-bank apartment obediently led the Gestapo to their door in the middle of the night. His parents were taken away and he never saw them or heard anything about them again. Each time he came for a session, he would stand in his underwear in front of me and point with his finger at all of the "defects" in his body of which Thérèse had made him aware: the right shoulder slightly higher and forward of the left; the hips rotated in a mirror fashion; a slight torsion in the knees; a depression in his right temple. Thérèse told him that I would be able to effect those alterations.

At the end of the day, Thérèse would regularly summon me into her office, having examined my clients after their sessions, in the manner of Rina's *lycée* martinets. She harshly criticized me for not manipulating these clients more rapidly into the symmetry which, in her mind, my Rolfing background should be able to bring about. In physical pain from the excessive number of sessions I was doing to support us and from the stress of living in a foreign culture, and in emotional pain from Thérèse's complaints, I would board the *métro* for the long ride home to our *quartier*. I would read in *Le Monde* of the growing number of savage attacks on young Jews in the working-class neighborhoods on the outskirts of the city. It was 1979, a time of growing racial and ethnic tensions. Swastikas were appearing more frequently among the graffiti. I felt sick at heart. On returning to our flat, bearing these many pains of the day, I would often find Elissa in foul humor, depressed by the onset of the crow's feet and sagging flesh of middle age, unable to stir up an interest in Aston-Patterning in Paris and becoming increasingly aware of how much she had subjected herself to the men in her life, of which I was the contemporary instance. Rina felt defeated by the rigid discipline and lack of kindness of the *lycée*, having been accustomed to the alternative schools and open classrooms of Santa Fe. It promised to be a bleak year, not at all the romantic Paris of our fantasies.

ONE OF OUR intentions in going to Europe was to get a sense of the history of our ancestors; I, by visiting their actual birthplaces; Elissa, by visiting the Jewish ghettoes in Western Europe, her family having originally come from Russia. I, more than Elissa, felt almost totally ignorant of my family's background, my grandparents never having wanted to talk about the Old Country.

On one excursion we went to Ireland to visit Kilbeggan, a small impoverished village where my Grandpa Joe had been born. In preparation, I read a number of books about Irish history about which I knew little; they made me angry. I learned how the British aristocracy had exploited religious differences between Roman Catholics and the Scotch Presbyterians, whom they imported to Northern Ireland four-hundred years ago. The fragmentation of the indigenous Irish made it easier for British landowners and industrialists to secure their interests. My anger intensified when we finally went there. In Kilbeggan, we found some of my distant relatives. Over long evening teas and gallons of Guinness, I learned the details of how our family and countless others had been repeatedly displaced from their farmlands by British landowners. I began to situate the broken spirit of Grandpa Joe and his relatives within a context larger than the oppressive heat and swamp fogs of the Sacramento Valley. As we traveled around the country, spending the nights in pubs talking with the locals, I found that younger, more secular-minded people wanted a unified Irish state. They were pessimistic of this ever happening because of the entrenched power of the Catholic Church, whose laws against contraception, divorce and abortion were written into Southern Irish law, making it unlikely that Protestants would ever agree to union. There was a general belief that the only hope for attaining peace and some kind of economic stability lay in a more secular approach to politics.

A week after we left, Pope John Paul arrived, touring the country like Mick Jagger, giving passionate sermons to crowds of hundreds of thousands, fanning the flames of Roman Catholic sectarianism, telling the people to continue to elect politicians who would support the Church-inspired laws. I felt rage at him and shame that, as a Jesuit, I had once vowed my allegiance to such a destructive crusade.

W HEN WE RETURNED TO PARIS, I had developed painful bursitis in my shoulders. Thérèse offered me a session of Mézieres work. She had me lie on a thin mat on the hardwood floor. For over two hours, she gave me directions about how I was to force my ankles, knees and elbows into exact alignment. She went over my body pushing and pulling various parts of it, trying to equalize right and left and to get my back flat on the hard surface of the floor. After repeated attempts to push my shoulders into alignment with her hands, she knelt on them, putting the full weight of her body into her knees. The bursitis became much worse.

❀

DURING THE ALL SAINTS DAY holidays, Elissa, Rina and I made our first visit to Rome. It was an uncanny feeling to come to a physical place for the first time feeling that I had spent a good part of my life there. Walking in the Forum, I could see Cicero orating before the Senate, Julius Caesar with Mark Antony and Brutus, Saint Paul in chains writing the letters which helped shape my childhood imagination. There was the Church of the Gesu where Ignatius had written the Rule that had shaped me as a Jesuit. In the background were my imaginings of Horace's music, Fellini's pageants, the bleakness of *The Bicycle Thief.*

Prepared by years of fantasy, I was awakened early on Sunday morning by the church bells pealing throughout the city calling me, I felt sure, to new mystical experiences. I set out alone by foot from our Trastevere pensione for Saint Peter's Basilica while Elissa and Rina remained asleep. The size of Saint Peter's oppressed me, more a symbol of immense power than of the spaciousness of spirit. An old cardinal was saying mass in the distance, with tourists walking around gossiping. I left, walking from church to church looking for something "spiritual." I found only gilded ceilings proclaiming the triumphal entry of the Church into world politics through the beneficence of Constantine, old men bent over the altars in heavy gold brocades, small groups of old women huddled submissively in the cavernous spaces below. By one o'clock in the afternoon, feet aching and soul black, I stumbled by chance into the ruins of Caracalla's baths, a few hundred yards away from the blood-stained Coliseum. I was flooded by images and feelings of the unity among the caesars, the popes, metropolitans, ayatollahs, generals and party chairmen, all blurring into one another: old men and their syncophants, detached from sensuous life and fascinated by power which was rationalized by complex abstract ideas, contemptuous of the earth-based spiritual practices of native peoples, served by tamed women.

The bursitis in my shoulders had become so severe that I couldn't lift my hands more than a few inches nor sleep on my sides. The pain lasted for a year.

In the course of attempting to heal it when we returned to Paris, I had my first experience with the Feldenkrais method called "Functional Integration." It was with Myriam Pfeffer, a sixty-year-old Polish Jew with homes in Paris and Tel Aviv. Her work felt kind. She would gently take my forearm and rotate it ever so slowly in its socket, letting the direction be guided by where my arm itself wanted to move. She seemed to be wringing out the pain that was saturating the shoulder bursa. She worked with my spinal column and ribs in that same way. She would take hold of the spinous process on each vertebra and rotate it ever so slightly, without force, just as far as I wanted it to go. It was very pleasurable. I never felt that she was forcing my body parts into preconceived locations where she *thought* they belonged, independently of who I was. She was helping me move where I actually wanted to move, but hadn't been able to locate how to do on my own. Over several months, her manipulations succeeded in relieving the pain and enabled me to move my shoulders again.

❧

DURING THE 1979 High Holy Days of our first months in Paris, the Jewish synagogue near the Arc de Triomphe was bombed. In the course of the year, there were frequent bombings of shops in the Jewish quarter along the *rue des Rosiers*. Interviewed on television one night, an eighty-year-old Jewish woman born in Paris was asked why she thought there had been this resurgence of anti-Semitism. "No resurgence," she replied, "it's just like always."

❧

I MADE A TRIP by myself to Norway to get a sense of the land where Grandpa Jul had been born and raised, hoping to get a better understanding of my father's side of the family. I prepared for it by reading Scandinavian history and folktales. I was surprised to find myself feeling the same kind of sadness during that journey as I do when I am walking through the old ghettoes of Venice or Rome or hiking in the old Indian lands in America where I have a sense of the brutal devastation of older, more humane cultures.

Riding ferries through the narrow fjords, I could easily imagine trolls and hobgoblins lurking in the moss-curtained crevasses. The mists coming up through breaks in the escarpments, followed by sunbursts and heavy rains, created a different sense of reality than I had in the drier sun-baked vistas of Southern France, Italy and California. It was easy to understand how the earliest form of democracy, still surviving in Iceland's Thing, would have been a natural development here. Before the advent of engine-driven boats, automobiles and helicopters, it must have been impossible to impose by armed force a single rule on the inverted cupcake like terrain. Villages, which are a few miles apart as the crow flies, are even now separated by water and auto journeys of several hours. It had to have taken a rare combination of greed and missionary zeal for the Catholic armies to wreak their savage destruction of the old religion and democracy, their depredations being completed by the Protestants.

In the museum of Thor Hyerdahl, whom I had previously known only through the film "Kon-Tiki," I discovered a new and inspiring slant on the Viking tradition. His life's work had consisted in gathering people from many countries to make boats according to ancient technologies, then to sail together propelled only by the wind and currents. One section of the museum was dedicated to the Ra, which had been constructed and sailed on the Indian Ocean by a crew of men from Mexico, the United States, the USSR, Italy, Egypt, Chad, Japan and Morocco. Written on the walls over the display of its history were these words:

"The voyages of the Ra proved that people with different colored skins, language, religious and political beliefs are able to work together towards a common objective." Hyerdahl and his crew had finally burned the boat on the shores of Eritrea to protest the savage civil war that had just broken out there.

I was beginning to get a new appreciation for the heritage of the Viking explorers—my father proudly kept a carved figure of one on his desk. I knew, of course, that they raped and pillaged like the Romans, British, Spanish and French. But there was an important difference: the Vikings succeeded by immersing themselves in other cultures. Like my grandparents, they gave up their language and ethnic customs to the point where they became indistinguishable from the native inhabitants. I even discovered in Bergen that the atypical jet black hair and dark skin of Grandpa Jul and my father's sister Charlotte were common among a strain of descendants from Viking sailors who had intermarried with Africans during the Moorish period.

Those days in Norway gave me a broader context for understanding certain earthy tendencies that I had glimpsed in my father and Grandpa Jul. Though baptized Lutherans, neither had much use for formal religion. But they did have what you might call a natural spirituality. Hunting and fishing in the wilderness, good times with one's family and friends and honesty in one's business dealings were the most important things to them. They didn't have much use for corrupt politicians, abstract ideologies and big schemes for making money. Unlike my rigid Irish relatives, my father had an easy sensuality. His remarks to my mother, even in his late seventies, were peppered with eroticism, winking at her as he made references to their taking showers together and to the back massages she gave him when he was sick. He felt at home in the natural world and often railed against those who were destroying it for the sake of greed. Throughout his life, he loved to cook and even had a recipe for pheasant stew published in *Sunset Magazine's* "Chefs of the West." During his last four years, he spent most of his time gardening, wood-carving and sitting in the yard watching the birds and squirrels.

Shortly after I returned from Norway to Paris, he and my mother came for a visit. One day, I drove them to Chartres. As my mother and I walked about the Cathedral, in awe of the walls of stained glass and the maze of bas reliefs on the stone walls, my father seemed to be getting progressively more upset, until he finally exploded into an angry tirade about how this monument could only have been built at the cost of an enormous staff of slave labor in the service of feudal lords and bishops. At that moment, I grasped how deeply Protestantism had permeated his guts, not formal Lutheranism, but an older anti-hierarchical, populist spirit, of which Martin Luther and Karl Marx were only more recent instances. I was reminded of the many times I had sat at home in his presence listening to him read the paper, hearing him rail year after year against the injustices of lying politicians and greedy, scheming businessmen. I had the humbling realization that my writing was merely a more learned version of the protests he had always been uttering against topsy-turvy social values. I had gained a theological, philosophical and sociological language to express what he so opposed in crude phrases, based on raw intuition. I had succeeded in getting that language thanks to his hard-earned money and encouragement to go to college.

When I published my second book, *Body*,[40] two years later, I had its dedication read: "To my father, a *p*rotestant," lower case.

THE DRAMA OF those various journeys punctuated the emotionally frustrating and physically painful day-to-day work in Thérèse's studio. Having already gone through the first unravelings of Rolf dogmatism in situations like I described with the Hopi and the Japanese-American women, I was giving less weight to how the visual structure of my clients deviated from the Template and more attention to their individuality. I looked at them more carefully as they came into my office and listened for the nuances in the tones

of their voices and the peculiar phrases they used in their spontaneous stories. I was learning to take in the many qualities of sensations of contact between the palm of my hand and their bodies.
I asked them for more feedback as we worked. The weightiness
of sensation drew me closer to people, reducing the distance created
by conceptually judging what was best for them independently of
their specific points of view. I was being drawn to work—albeit
non-verbally, with my hands—more in the style of a good psychotherapist who is trained to pay careful attention to the nuances
of the world of his or her clients, and to help the client gain access
to his or her own healing capacities.

That is not what Thérèse wanted from me, nor did some of
the clients whom she had assigned to me. I was to be the heavy
artillery to assault the structural deformities that were impervious
to her Mézieriste Praxiteles-inspired forays.

I heaved and hauled on the massive body of the Duc de
Querçize. It was eerie when my fingertips came up against the
sacs of shrapnel embedded in the muscles of his arms, legs and
abdomen. I didn't know what I was doing there. It seemed point-
less—and physically impossible—for me to move his lumbar spine
where Thérèse wanted it. Nor could I find another point of contact
between us which might give me a clue to some other purpose for
our work. Like one of Proust's Guermantes, he was very concerned
to let me know about his aristocratic lineage, his family estates,
his intimate connections to the art of the Louvre. He spoke to me
as if I might have been his hairdresser. He regularly put off pay-
ments, saying that he did not ordinarily carry money. He did not
come for his final appointment and never reimbursed me for our
several sessions of work.

I was able to establish a more human contact with Charles, the
couturier. I found myself fascinated by his stories about his own
history. He became open with me about his life with his wife and
daughters. Because of his childhood experience with anti-Semitism in Paris, he and his wife had shaped their bodies, gestures
and clothing to be of anonymous ethnicity. As part of that quest for

anonymity, they were planning to have nose operations for their two teenage daughters so that no one would suspect that they were Jewish. In the course of those stories, he spoke of how much he was troubled by bursitis in his shoulders, which seriously interfered with his sewing. Familiar with his pain from the inside, I was able to succeed in relieving it for him, and subsequently for his wife.

Like the women in Santa Fe, Abdul Shaalan eluded the furthest reaches of my rational knowing. I could not grasp what it was like to be Muslim or to have been tortured by one's own countrymen and fellow believers. The tonicity and textures of his flesh were puzzling to me. The familiar goals of structural alignment, improving the range of movement in the joints, and reduction of overall stress did not seem relevant. Once again I was forced to turn to something more primal. Yet here, that primal was not so much fleshy as it was verbal. As I carefully touched him and moved his limbs, I let myself speak to him quietly about Nasser, Sadat and the Sandinistas, with whom he was now involved. We spoke about our shared hopes for a better future. I experienced a closeness with him, which seemed to have some value to him. It was a particular kind of conversation, quiet, slow, close to the gut, touching and healing the wounded flesh.

My work with Françoise was also like that. Her history had left her so cynical about any system of values or meanings that I felt helpless to do anything about her despair other than to stay there with her, touching her as she spoke about it and helping her breathe into feelings about it. Trying to affect changes in her body alignment seemed both unnecessary and irrelevant to her attempts to find some glimmer of light in the dark forests of her memories.

In 1980 I sent Thomas Hanna, editor of the journal *Somatics*, a draft of an article in which I argued that the use of visual ideal images of the body, specific "character types" and preconceived plans for manipulation based on such concepts, encouraged dependency and self-doubt in clients of Somatic therapy, and hampered the creativity of Somatic practitioners. He asked me to add to the article a response to this question: if one abandons the organizing principle of external ideals, character types and manipulative recipes, how might one organize one's work and teach others? I appended to the article, titled "Somatic Platonism," a sketch of a plan for educating Somatic therapists grounded in a study of the law-abiding processes that are inherent in our bodies: genetic, neurophysiological, anatomical, physical, psychological, social and spiritual.[41] During the past thirteen years I have been implementing and filling out that vague outline under the pressures of developing the first graduate school program in Somatics.

SARTRE DIED IN the spring of 1980 towards the end of our stay in Paris. I had thought of him frequently during that year, as I experienced first-hand the scars left by the many idealisms which had ravaged Europe over the centuries. Thérèse constantly criticized me for failing to align the people she sent me, complaining that I was probing too deeply into their interior lives. Most of my clients, virtually all of whom had been affected by torture or war, wanted from me not an exploration of more primal and healing ways of living, but cosmetic improvements in bodily form. Rina could hardly bear leaving for school in the morning because of the abusiveness of her teachers. Elissa had created a secret life in Paris in reaction to her terror of growing old with her increased awareness of what she had given up to be in two marriages and a mother. Our immersion in the European scars of war and racism had rekindled her lifelong political passions to the point that she had decided to give herself completely to the anti-nuclear movement on our return to the U.S.

Our marriage held all the complex strands of the 1960s, its utopian visions of a better world, its psychedelic breakdown of rigid intellectual categories, and its turn towards the body, combined with a reckless lack of boundaries. The sexual, intellectual and political passions that brought us together and fired our creative marriage for ten years were fast being eroded by lack of trust and resentments that were older than either of us. She began to see me only as an embodiment of all the men who had made her personal life miserable and who were traumatizing the planet. I found her dangerous, another woman who, like my mother, Ida Rolf and Thérèse, threatened to devour my sense of self in her own oceanic psyche.

In that Sartrean bleakness, Elissa, Rina and I returned to the United States and immediately moved from Santa Fe to San Francisco, where we struggled unsuccessfully to rebuild a shared life. Although our marriage unraveled over a period of four years of heart-wrenching pain, we eventually found our way back to our friendship and the shared vision of life which had originally brought us together. In our last months together, we often took walks or went to dinner and were able to speak intimately about our unsuccessful struggles to develop new relationships and our continuing work as writers and practitioners of Somatics.

In April 1985, just four days after I had left for Denmark to begin a three-month teaching stint at various centers throughout Europe, Elissa was run down and killed by a drunk and stoned motorcyclist who was being pursued by the police in Berkeley. I immediately flew back to San Francisco. It was the first time in my life that violence had come so close to my heart. During the following weeks, I was deluged by a constant barrage of images of the details of the intense violence that had crushed her—the roaring bike, the police cars in hot pursuit with their sirens wailing, her emerging from Naomi Newman's car, stepping out into College Avenue, her sudden glance at what was coming, the thoughts in her mind, her final sensations. My pain at her death broke down many of the interior walls that had blinded me to the relative value of things: the ultimate significance of tending to my simple relationships with loved ones, and the relative unimportance of most of my daily obsessions about money, work and national politics.

After a few weeks, I flew back to Copenhagen to resume my work in Europe. I had to take a train to Paris and eventually Vienna. That four-day ride through Western Europe coincided with the week of memorial services for the two World Wars. Reagan was making his "let-bygones-be-bygones" visit to Bitburg. Sitting on the train in that peculiar openness of spirit that comes with intense grief, I passed countless cemeteries filled with Europeans remembering their war dead. Thinking of what a high percentage of people in the world had been directly touched by physical violence to their loved ones, I knew for the first time in my flesh what that was like and how absent from my viewpoint had been the traces of that commonplace reality. My wife's death and that train ride created a wound that opened for me the heart of the universe.

Male Vociferousness

UNLIKE THE BODY-SPIRIT ecosystems of culture and politics, gender had been more invisible to me. "Man" and "woman" seemed as natural as the sun and moon.

I spent nearly three decades within an exclusively male ghetto. Before joining the Jesuits, I had gone to an all-male high school and university. For most of fourteen years in the Jesuits, my only contact with women was an occasional visit with my mother and with the few women who were visiting on exclusively male-college campuses. At Yale, before the undergraduate college had gone coed, there were only a handful of women students in the philosophy department and not a single woman professor. From the time I graduated from elementary school in 1947 until 1971, when I had completed my doctorate, I had not been assigned to read a single book authored by a woman, nor did I seek one out. I had never even known a woman physician, lawyer or dentist.

Then in the extremist pattern characteristic of my life, I angrily rejected the world of men and gave myself almost exclusively to the emotional and intellectual world of women. There were Elissa, Ida Rolf and Thérèse, passionately idealistic, strong-willed and often abusive. Within the field of Somatics, I chose only to study with women: Judith Aston, Emilie Conrad Da'Oud, Bonnie Cohen and Charlotte Selver. I deliberately avoided the easy contact I might have had with geniuses like Moshe Feldenkrais and Stanley Keleman. Until I was well into writing this book, I saw only women for psychotherapy. My closest friendships were with women. When we moved from Santa Fe to San Francisco in 1980 and I returned to the intellectual life, I immersed myself in feminist literature. Doing so brought to the surface all my old resentments of men — of my father, Church and Jesuit authorities, and the secular madmen who had ravaged history. My male friendships suffered from hard-edged competitiveness and a lack of emotional connection. I distrusted male authorities.

I finally woke up to the obvious fact that the distrust and resentment were just as much directed against myself, after all, a man. Reaching a healing point of view required me to come to grips with my own maleness. There have been many aspects of masculinity which I have had to address in overcoming my alienation, most of which have been described in great detail by other writers on gender. In addition, there has been the daunting trial of having to come to terms with a peculiar quality of male voice.

Of all the qualities that make up the male shaping of the world, I have been dominated by one strong image. It is of a drone of male voices as constant as the traffic hum in a big city; men speaking in disconnected ways about what they thought it was important for us to hear, seeming to have little sense of us there, too; men taking charge of conversations at the dinner table; priests, ministers, old and New Age gurus explaining the cosmos and morality; teachers, psychologists, political experts, philosophers, administrators and just ordinary working men telling it the way it is. That urge to speak a particular story is a testosterone-driven storm whose roar drowns out the voices of women, soft-spoken men, children, bears, dolphins and sequoias. The roar of its relentless, unpredictable tides makes it hard to tell different stories.

I hear that voice in myself all the time, regularly noticing that I am talking too much, that I interrupt others in a rush to get the floor, adding layer upon layer of force to my words so that people will realize how crucial they are. My urge to speak often seems

out of my control no matter how much meditation, psychotherapy and body therapy I do. It constantly disrupts my relations with
my loved ones, my colleagues and my students, who complain that
my voice makes them feel insignificant, dismissed or stupid.

Even as a child, I was bewildered by radically competing ideas
about reality associated with different kinds of male voices.

My education in spiritual matters had been signed over by my
father to my mother in a contract the Church demands as a condition for non-Catholics who wanted to marry Catholics. I learned
as a young child that only Catholics had access to ultimate truth. I
grew up with the perverse belief that my non-churchgoing father
was ignorant of things of the spirit, at worst even willfully turning
away from them. Although I learned that people of good will
might get into heaven if they lived moral lives and really believed
that their religion was correct, my father's case was special. Because
he had been exposed to the fullness of Catholic truth by living
with my mother and Grandpa Joe, I always doubted that he could
be of good will, rejecting as he did this intimate contact with truth.
I justified his behavior by telling myself that he was just ignorant,
even though evidence pointed to a more deliberate—and evil—
denial. He always made a show of refusing to eat fish with us on
Fridays, even though he always ordered it when we went out to
dinner on other days. He made a point of sleeping in on Sundays
when my mother, Grandpa Joe and I would go to mass, and he
had a thinly veiled contempt for Irish-born celibate priests in black
gowns forbidding married people to practice birth control. And
there was his anger, one of the seven deadly sins.

My father's voice was like a loose gun, out of kilter with other
aspects of his personality which were unusually humane. It fired in
unpredictable rages. Although he never hit my mother or me, a
bullet-like intensity in his voice would leave me feeling wounded,
or a mean tone shriveled me up. Grandpa Jul and my uncles spoke
like that to my grandmother, aunts and cousins. And there was a
nasty quality in their voices, their mouths tightening when they
spoke about Blacks, Jews and Mexicans.

Often, as a boy, I would be furious with my father who had just stalked out of the room after a sadistic outburst of anger at me or my mother that appeared out of nowhere. My mother would try to comfort me by making excuses for him time after time, saying how much he loved us, how his anger had nothing to do with us but was due to the hard life he lived to support us. She told me how hard it had been for him to start working as a handyman for his father, Grandpa Jul, a housebuilder, when he was only eleven years old. Except for a few years during the Great Depression when their business failed, he worked with Jul in that trade until World War II. I could see that Grandpa Jul was always yelling angrily at him, and he was always sullen and cowed around Grandpa Jul.

That aspect of my father's voice seemed particularly strange because he was otherwise so loving. Many men write of how distant their fathers have been; as I immersed myself in gender literature and psychotherapy, I came to believe that mine was, too. But in retrospect, that is not accurate. I have photos taken at Santa Cruz when I was four years old that remind me of how much affection I felt from him during those years. One photo was taken in a booth at the penny arcade, with him holding me close so that we can both fit into the frame. In another, we are making sand castles together on the beach, one of my happiest childhood memories. Although he regularly had to work out of town, he would take me with him and give me little tasks to do on the job, like replenishing the water jugs for his work crews. I often spent school vacations away with him on his jobs, living in hot ramshackle motels on the outskirts of small towns. He took me on hunting and fishing trips with him and his friends. When he was home, he always engaged with me, playing board games, bicycling around Land Park, even joining me in my favorite occupation of listening to radio serials. He was always generous with me. When I had fantasies of being a cowboy he even bought me a horse; it scared me, and I didn't ride it very much.

It was that very closeness that made his hostile outbursts so confusing. While some men tell of how distanced they were by their fathers' anger, I felt submerged in it, like I had gone under a breaker on top of which I had been body-surfing a moment before. One minute smiling and friendly, the next minute his rage exploded from his angry eyes.

Despite those signs of ignorance and ill-will, his voice exuded certainty. He gave passionate talks at the dinner table about the evils of trade unions and the encroachment of Blacks and Chicanos in our neighborhood. He aggressively controlled what anyone was allowed to say, who was allowed to talk, and for how long. Very few subjects were admitted for conversation—the weather, gossip about friends and relatives. If my mother dared to raise an issue that he disliked, by, for example, objecting to Harry Truman's unprecedented 1946 injunction prohibiting the steelworker's union from striking, he would immediately halt the conversation, proclaiming that as a housewife she had no knowledge of what the unions were doing and should therefore keep her mouth shut about the issue. My mother quietly went about her business of eating and clearing the dishes, never speaking back to him.

Non-churchgoing Grandpa Jul and my anti-Catholic uncles, none of whom had any education beyond high school, spoke with that same authoritative tone about what was real, no matter whether it involved politics, religion, science or any subject imaginable. They, like my father, were aggressive speakers, rarely paying attention to anyone else, intruding, interrupting, always trying to direct the flow of communication. Or they withdrew into sullen silence. My aunts Gladys and Charlotte provided a thread of sanity in my childhood sense of the world. Although they never spoke back to the men, they provided a quiet background of sarcastic and humorous distance about men's claims on truth with their glances and quiet jokes out of the men's earshot.

Throughout all the years I spent with those men in the family, I cannot remember a single conversation in which we were engaged in a shared inquiry, posing various opinions, weighing them, seriously considering the other's point of view, suggesting modifications. These men typically resolved debate about controversial questions by a decree that we women and children were stupid and did not understand what they asserted was the "real" world.

Like Catholic arcana, their world held a sense of mystery to me, an unknown "outside" beyond the physical safety of our quiet house, a larger realm in which my father built dams on raging rivers in the high Sierras and cut pipelines through the hot Nevada desert with heavy equipment which often injured a man. It was off limits to women and physically weak men. When my father proudly took me into it, I never found a practicing Roman Catholic there. "Reality" seemed to be the exclusive option of non-religious working men who played squash at the Elks Club, swam and showered together naked, and sat afterwards in the bar, drinking and smoking, talking with great ease about business deals and city politics.

I want to underscore the fact that the compelling claims these men made on reality had nothing to do with the kinds of things we usually associate with substantiating such claims—evidence, ingenuity, experience, wit and logic—but were based simply on an authoritative quality of speaking, which conveyed an unswerving assumption of power.

The vigor of their speaking cast doubt on the reliability of the contrasting Catholic story, which was told with such reticence. The voice of my mother's Roman Catholic father, Grandpa Joe, was different from that of my father and Grandpa Jul: he hardly spoke at all and then only meekly. His voice seemed snuffed out by the peculiar circumstances of his life. His mother had died giving birth to him in Kilbeggan. He was brought across the Atlantic to New York, then by train across the United States to Sacramento by his older sisters when he was only two years old, and raised by them and his aunts. That was in 1880. He went on to marry a daughter of Sacramento pioneers—her portrait always hung in our home—who died as a young woman when my mother was only twelve. By the time I was born he seemed to have been rendered speechless by that history. He lived with us in a tiny den, which my father grudgingly converted into a bedroom for him when poverty forced him to sell his own house. He went off to work as a salesman at a haberdashery, came home and sat quietly reading the paper and listening to baseball on the radio. He went to church at the Cathedral of the Blessed Sacrament and to Sacramento Solon baseball games. He puttered about in my father's woodshop. Sometimes on Sundays he went off for enigmatic trysts with women. That was all he did. He never said much, rarely laughed or got angry or had any friends. Even though it was hard for me to find a personal connection with him in his silence, he was kind and gentle unlike my father and Grandpa Jul. And he didn't belittle my mother or make jokes about Jews and Blacks.

The tentativeness in his voice was reflected in the voices of our Catholic parish. In contrast to the booming voices I could hear walking past the Lutheran and Seventh Day Adventist churches, the Cathedral congregation sang in such flimsy tones, and you could hardly make out the words of their responses to the priest at Mass. The official voice of the Church was embodied in the Cathedral pastor, Monsignor Renwald, who seemed to have trouble standing upright in the pulpit while he gave sermons about eternal joy in tired and meek tones.

As I grew older, religious teachers would directly address those vocal confusions. To become effective missionaries for the Word, we had to learn how to speak with authority, miming the Biblical God who is verbose like the men in my family, thundering down angrily from mountain tops, dictating endless tracts, apparently deaf to the fact that many simply don't care, and many others are in too much pain to listen. Learning to speak like that version of God was the centerpiece of our Jesuit training. Speech training was the only course given every year throughout Jesuit training. In the two-year Novitiate where most of our time was given to meditation, silent work and prayer, the only secular study was rhetoric. Not even Biblical study got that honor. We practiced sounding cadences, varying tone of voice, combined the use of gesture and posture for effect. Our models were Demosthenes who learned to speak by filling his mouth with pebbles and outdoing the roar of the Aegean, and Cicero, whose five-hundred-word cadences we imitated in practice Latin sermons to our brothers. We studied the speeches of the great Christian orators like John Chrysostom ("golden tongue") and Philip Neri. There was little concern about the rationality of content, its evidence or logic. We were to focus on the emotionally evocative power of certain combinations of words, with sonorous vowels, rolled out in a certain tone, to evoke devotion and belief in the listeners. We were often spurred on by Nietzsche's dictum: "If these men want me to believe in their saviour, they will have to look more like men who have been saved!" Some of our teachers even had a fascination with Hitler. Although they identified him as diabolic, they studied the techniques he used to sway masses of people, so that we could use those same techniques in service of the truthful Word.

The Jesuit philosophy of rhetoric was not dialogical, conversational in nature, but dominant-submissive in form. Although our community life involved intimate conversations among all ages and levels of Jesuits, the formal structure of speaking-listening was like that in my childhood home. We listened to countless lectures on spirituality without being offered the chance to raise a single question. The characteristic pedagogy during our long education in humanities, philosophy and theology primarily involved lectures with virtually no time for questions or discussions. The only formal opportunities for being listened to were in the confessional and in meetings with the spiritual advisor. But those were like speaking with Grandpa Joe; there was no give and take, just talking to a passive listener who gave little response, if any.

When I left the religious for the secular world, I found the speaking-listening structure basically unchanged. The Yale philosophy courses were primarily dull lectures by scholars who seemed to have little concern that there were other intelligent adults in the room. When a cadre of us in the heady spirit of the late 1960s organized to change the quality of dialogue within classes and seminars in the department, a psychiatrist was brought in to explain to us the dynamics of our unclarified parental hostility. One of the faculty explained to us that we were mistaken in thinking that the job of the department was to educate philosophers. In fact, he argued, its task was to train teachers of philosophy, namely men who had learned to speak the restricted language of the academy, addressing the appropriate subjects, writing according to the authoritative canons.

That intimate bond between voice and truth is not confined to the cloister and academy. It is the dominant authority of voice in our political leaders, medical experts, ministers and other authorities—not data, reasonableness or authenticity—that wins popular support. If you look at extreme cases like Hitler, Stalin, Castro, Mao and Pol Pot you find that their overwhelming authority over masses of people is typically associated with a vocal hypnotic manipulation of the most primitive emotions. And in our supposedly more civilized politics, you find presidents, generals and ousted police chiefs speaking not out of reason but sentimentalism, making sloppy—even tearful—appeals to ill-defined patriotism as well as racist innuendoes, and playing on citizens' worst fears.

I HAD FOUND many sources of healing among women—friends, lovers and therapists—who were able to listen to me and respect me. But in this task of healing my rift with men, particularly with my father, I had to find out where there were sources of healing and wisdom among men. When I finally raised that question for myself, I noticed that there were a handful of men along the way who gave me hints of another kind of masculine speaking and listening: religious men, psychologists, native Americans.

A few of my Jesuit college teachers had strong voices, claiming an even more compelling hold on "the real" than did my father and uncles. But besides speaking with deep and passionate tones about transforming the world, they also actively listened to me. Their facial expressions as well as their words showed they were affected by me, that we were actually conversing in a way that was new to me. More than other factors, it was their capacity to listen that eventually drew me to their celibate way of life. No one before, neither men nor women, had listened to me the way they did. Moreover, the quality of their speaking and listening radiated an affection for each other that I had never seen among other adult men; they actually conversed. And they also listened to women, Jews, Blacks and Chicanos.

Being listened to was delicious. It was a foretaste of what I experienced more fully in Somatics, enticing me into prolific wetlands of reality that are normally obscured by the scrub-brush of speech. Being heard gave me a sense of myself as fleshy "all the way through," with coursing blood, pulsing organs and lungs, instead of feeling that I was a brittle muscular container filled with ghostly conversations. That sense of "all the way thoroughness" provided a lifeline to a rock-solid promontory of reality where I would eventually come ashore after floating adrift for many years as "an old man's staff."

I ENCOUNTERED CARL ROGERS and his associates in the early 1960s. Unlike all the men who had drawn me up to then, he looked plain in every way: no costume, Midwestern accent, ordinary face, married with children, son of a Methodist minister who himself had turned from religion as inhumane. His philosophy of Client-Centered Psychotherapy and Education was equally plain, with no technical terms linked by an esoteric web of propositions. The simplicity of his theory belied its revolutionary power. It goes like this: babies are born with a vast store of intelligence and creativity located in their cells. But because they are typically treated like blank slates, sometimes even as if they were intrinsically evil, they grow into adults who *feel* that they are stupid, or worse, evil. Psychotherapy, education and even businesses would work better, he argued, if therapists, teachers and executives learned to listen to their charges more carefully and respectfully. He encouraged these people to speak less, letting their words be motivated not so much by their own supposedly precious ideas but by responses generated by listening carefully to others.

I knew from the outset that, if this theory could be made to work, it could be a radical challenge to authoritarianism.

I naively approached my first Rogerian group as if I were going to a social gathering. I soon felt that I had stumbled into dangerous territory. There was too much silence; if I said anything, people actually listened. In that atmosphere of silence, I often heard myself babbling, trying desperately to keep up appearances, afraid that my demons, hidden under a veneer of politeness, would burst forth. But step by step, like going into a mountain lake on a summer morning, I found that the first chill of truthfulness and silence led to deep refreshment. I engaged in Rogerian-inspired groups throughout the 1960s, sometimes with a leader trained by Rogers and other times without a formal leader.

I first tried out Rogerian methods in an ethics class which I was teaching at Loyola University of Los Angeles in 1963. During the first week, I posed a number of complex moral issues to the students:

> You believe that the war in Vietnam is immoral, but that World War II was OK. Because your parents, pastor and Cardinal McIntyre say that the War is just and that Catholic men are obliged to serve, you don't qualify for CO status. What then?

> You get drunk at a party and have sex with a girl you don't know. You are poor, living in the barrio. She gets pregnant. Would you pay for her to have an abortion?

I recorded the responses which the students gave to the various dilemmas. For the rest of the semester, I played back their responses for them and had them reflect on what they had said. I was stunned by the results. They covered much more of "the material" than I would ever have attempted or asked them to study in standard textbooks. Their insights were as complex and subtle as any professional ethician's.

While I was completing pre-ordination studies of theology at the Jesuit Alma College in the Santa Cruz mountains in 1966, Carl Rogers was invited to bring his staff and conduct a weekend marathon for all 108 inhabitants including faculty, spiritual advisors, us students and lay brothers. Only Father Robert, a theology professor, refused to attend. That weekend of sitting together, divided into groups of ten, often spending long periods in silence, talking slowly and intimately about feelings, broke apart the structure of theology teaching. On the following Monday morning, the first day of a new academic quarter, we went to our first class on Trinitarian theology taught by Father Robert. A prim, carefully-stitched-together man, whose principal interests were bird-watching and the theology of infant baptism, he proceeded to outline each of our future classes and assignments. Pat, a 250-pound ex-trucker who was working as a counselor in San Francisco's Tenderloin bringing Christ to addicts and prostitutes, stood up and said: "You haven't even asked us what we *feel* like doing in this class. Everything you've said sounds like crap. The people I work with don't give a shit about how you can have three persons in one God." He walked out, slamming the door behind him. As if nothing had happened, Father Robert calmly proceeded to outline the course. An ordinarily quiet student, an artist, stood up sobbing and said, "You don't even care about what we feel, do you?" In the first sign of emotion I had ever seen in him, Father Robert slapped his hand on the desk and shouted, "God damn it, I am interested in you, but you're about to become priests and you've got to understand the Holy Trinity." Angry voices came from all around the room: "We're persons. We've got feelings. What difference does the Trinity make anyhow?" Quivering all over and flushed in the face, Father Robert stormed out of class.

You could hear doors slamming all over the campus, with faculty and students running hither and yon, some sobbing, some yelling at each other.

True to the spirit of our founder, Ignatius Loyola, who wanted us to be ready at a moment's notice to give up family and friends to follow the promptings of the Holy Spirit, the faculty regrouped at morning coffee and decided to embrace rather than resist Rogerian pedagogy. They each returned to their classes proposing to revise the entire theology curriculum—which happened to be in a post-Vatican Council mess anyway. Standard course content was thrown out. In every class, the teacher would henceforth interview the student to ascertain how his particular interests fit with the course's subject matter. On the basis of that interview, they would work out an individualized program of study. Any given course, say on the sacraments, might be divided into small interest groups: The Sacraments in the Ancient Greek Mystery Religions (for those of us who were experimenting with psychedelics), The Sacraments and Political Protest, The Sacraments and Sexuality, etc. The teacher would act like a Rogerian facilitator, indicating where we could find relevant sources and suggesting fruitful lines of research. He would give occasional lectures (optional attendance—another radical departure from seminary rules), and, of course, prepare a list of questions still required by Rome for examination of candidates for the priesthood. (A principle of Rogerian pedagogy was that most official exams were best prepared for as a specific task perhaps by oneself or by working in task-oriented study groups, not by encumbering a curriculum. In the case of priestly exams, the material was easily learned outside of the classroom.)

Students who were not planning to teach after ordination but to engage in some kind of community work, like Pat, were allowed to design courses related to their work, for example, doing research on drug-addiction and homosexuality in place of the former standardized course in moral theology.

That Rogerian model of listening-speaking became a hallmark of the post-Vatican Catholic Church. Parishes throughout America created networks of small groups of lay people discussing their problems among each other and with their pastors and nuns. The Sunday sermon often gave way to a dialogue between priest and parishioners. Small discussion groups began to be incorporated into formerly silent retreats. Even the Catholic bishops began to initiate such groups. Liberation theology, based on similar principles of egalitarian dialogue, was thriving in Latin America. But the inquisitional voice reasserted itself with even more virulence. Rome rapidly replaced the dean of our theology school with a young conservative who forbade Rogers to return for a follow-up weekend a year later.

For over two decades conservative bishops and theologians struggled to regain power, and finally succeeded with the 1978 election of the present Pope John Paul II. He has worked strenuously to stem the tide of the conversational attack on centralized authority, taking every opportunity to replace Vatican II bishops with conservatives who support the old vociferousness.

Bonnie bainbridge cohen says that resolving puzzles about experiences of speaking and listening were crucial in developing her Somatics method of Body-Mind Centering. I first became aware of the unusual results of her work at the end of a week-long study seminar in which she, I and a handful of other teachers had engaged. At the close of the seminar, we all stood and joined hands in a circle, and remained quietly together for some minutes. Bonnie, a frail and short woman, was standing next to me. Suddenly, she let out a roar that nearly shattered my bones. It might have come from a person three times her size. "I had to clear out the accumulated stress," she said, quietly apologetic.

She argues that the kind of hearing that we typify as "letting things go in one ear and out the other" is directly linked with a kind of speaking that is detached from the whole person. "I learned to talk late and then stuttered until grade school. I will still do so occasionally when I am tired or verbally stressed. I spelled the way I heard, uncertainly. In seventh grade, while taking music appreciation, I couldn't tell if the pitch was going up or down unless the tones were widely spaced, and I couldn't differentiate the string instruments from the woodwinds.

"When Erick Hawkins challenged me on my voice, my voice had a monotone quality, a range of about 1.25 octaves, was barely audible and expressed little emotion. After twenty years of focusing on my voice, my voice is louder and more solid, there is more fluctuation of pitch, my range is about two octaves, and *I can express more easily how I feel emotionally.*"[42]

Len Cohen is Bonnie's husband, a grizzly bear of a man, 6 feet 3 inches tall, about 220 pounds, a chiropractor, father with Bonnie of three children. In 1971, he and Bonnie were living in Tokyo so that he could study with an aikido master. To earn a living, Bonnie had taken on the job of developing an occupational therapy school for the Japanese government. At one stage of the course, Len was learning to use the four-foot staff, thrusting, parrying and counter-thrusting with a partner. Part of the exercise required learning how to coordinate vocal sounds with breath and the movements of the body. One day, with his master as his partner, he found his voice joined so intimately with other parts of his body that its strength hurled his master to the ground before the staff even touched him. When he returned home, he was sitting at the kitchen table telling Bonnie about the incident when suddenly he heard a sonorous voice. Not recognizing it, he said, with a start: "Who in the hell is saying that?" Recognizing in an instant that it was coming from him, he then said, "How am I doing that?" He says in retrospect that the best way to describe it was not "I made a sound," but "sound was coming out." In the next moment, he became disconcerted by the feeling of the uncontrollable nature of the sound. In those short moments of distanced reflection, that profound voice left him and has never returned.

I TELL THESE vignettes about Carl Rogers and the Cohens to give a sense of the intricacies required to fuse voice with the gut, heart, lungs and imagination. As monks and shamans in all the spiritual traditions have known for centuries, the linkage between voice and spirit is forged at the cost of long years of chanting, breathing and sensory awareness. Even then, there remains the most difficult task of linking the voice with the heart. I had to face the fact that the conversational problems raised in this chapter cannot be solved by a "change of mind." Despite my ideals of kindness and respect for people, especially for those who have been oppressed, I continually found myself speaking oppressively. I have had to keep with the hard tasks of learning how to breathe and slow down when someone signals me that I am speaking too overpoweringly or sharply. In such moments, I also have to cope with my tendencies to justify my behavior. Somatics therapies and meditation have helped me learn how to slow down and turn my energies from their normal course of rapid and narcissistic inner dialogue towards a felt connection with others. Psychotherapy has weakened my defensiveness, and kept me from being defeated by past failures to engage in attempts to love.

It was not until my father died that I was able to heal the scars between us. That healing was associated with my coming to understand the spiritual dimension of his physically and emotionally angry voice.

He was seventy-eight years old, at the end of an unusually peaceful few years during which he had been relatively free of the health crises that had plagued him for a decade. He and my mother had recently moved from the house he had built downtown in 1939 to a house near Land Park, an easier neighborhood in a different part of Sacramento. The new house was more spacious and light, with a big garden and friendly neighbors, a short walk from Holy Spirit Church. Although his health had stopped him from playing sports at the Elks Club and he had stopped drinking and playing cards, he continued to go there to take showers. When I seemed puzzled by that, he did an atypical thing of taking the care to explain himself in a calm and direct tone of voice. He said that he liked doing it because the shower-room, where men were together naked with their surgical and war scars in plain sight, was the only place where they told the truth. Two months earlier, he and my mother had flown to Kauai to celebrate their fifty-fifth wedding anniversary. Shortly after, they attended my second wedding. He was pleased by the perception, mistaken it turned out, that I had finally entered into a successful marriage (it lasted only a year). For this brief time, he and I were easy with each other. He appreciated that I had dedicated my book, *Body*, to him.

On the July Fourth weekend, 1986, my new wife Lauren and I drove up from San Francisco to Sacramento. On the Fourth, my father barbecued steaks for us and a couple of our family's lifelong friends. The day after, the four of us rode through the foothills of the Sierras. In response to my offers, he vigorously insisted on driving. As we passed Folsom and Plymouth enroute to Jackson, he talked incessantly, but feelingly, without the usual edge of anger, about his childhood memories of those foothills. As a young boy, he had worked there doing odd jobs in his uncle's gold mines, then later with Grandpa Jul on various water projects. Twenty-five years earlier, he had spent months in that region unsuccessfully searching for the body of my twenty-year-old cousin who had disappeared going over a waterfall on the Consumnes River. Returning at dusk to the city, we had Italian spaghetti at a restaurant a few blocks from where both he and my mother had been born. Uncharacteristically, he ate very little and spoke easily, not trying to control the flow of conversation. When Lauren and I arose early on Monday morning, he was already fully dressed, having gone for a walk and looking unusually happy. He had not been angry the entire weekend. As we were leaving, he called me aside and said that it had been very important for him to drive the day before, his last words to me. After we left for San Francisco, he drove by himself to the Elks Club, took off his clothes to get into the shower and dropped dead.

Lauren and I immediately drove back. It was over one-hundred degrees. My father had meticulously prepared for his death except for getting a grave, so my mother and I had to go around in our grief and shock in the extreme heat dealing with vulture-like grave salesmen. At one point, I had my mother rest while I continued the shopping. When I returned home, their pastor had left a message asking me if I would say some words at the funeral mass. I said to my mother that I couldn't, I was in shock, I would not be able to speak without breaking down, and I had long ago given up the pulpit. But I had the strange experience of being physically unable to pick up the phone to call him to refuse. It was as if an unseen hand were holding my wrist.

I got into the shower weepy and collapsed in grief. As the water refreshed me, I was suddenly flooded by memories of times when my father had been angry. But this time it was different from the many times when I had just paid attention to the personal hostility towards my mother and myself, the pain and resentment I had harbored all my life about that. I recalled the day at Chartres when I saw him not just as an angry man, but as a protestant with deep feelings about the oppression of working people by bishops and dukes. I found myself straightening up out of my posture of grief impelled by a haunting dream-like rush of voices from deep inside. They seemed as if they were the booming voices of a vast horde of men coming out of the wet northern forests of Scandinavia far back in history; lodged within my cells, they were urging me into their lead, my father just behind me, his father and uncles and grandfathers just behind him. Their sonorous voices coursed through my blood, speaking to me about the importance of love for family and friends, care for the forests, clear waters and cool air of the fjords, about respect for reindeer, bald eagles and whales. It felt as if they were injecting images into my brain of what survival was like in those difficult climes with extremes of weather and lack of arable land. And of how many times they had to uproot themselves from family and land to go far afield to indenture themselves to feudal lords to make a living. Of how invading Christians from southern Europe worked to mute their vision, destroying the old nature religions and the earliest democracies.

The flood of images and voices was giving me a feeling for how those generations of spirit-men had been struggling for centuries with little success to find a voice. Their ancient stories, like native American and African stories, were too homely, talking of heart, corn, trout and hummingbirds. They were no match for the aggressive power of the disembodied philosophical, theological, scientific, technological and psychological verbosities that followed in the wake of foreign armies and the Industrial Revolution to shape the dominant mind-set of the modern world. Enraged by having been muted by those verbose invasions, they were left with the crude devices of yelling, pounding, lashing out in anger to get their words across.

After years of seeing my father's rage only within a Western psychological framework, I grasped something else. I saw him as the most recent before me of an ancient group of men trying to work their way out of flesh, mosses, soil and rocks, like the gigantic prisoners carved by Michelangelo in his old age, groping for words to liberate themselves from the stony prison of silence. They were angry that things were not right with the world. Frustrated by the pain of their lives and their impotence in reshaping reality, they talked too much, often lashing out at their wives and children, and then lapsed into the sullen and often drunken despair of guilt.

My father, with his high school education, did not have the words to make sense of such things. He lacked not only the knowledge and understanding of the larger picture but of the spiritual, psychological and Somatic practices that would teach him how to buck his testosterone storms, connecting his vision of a better life with his way of speaking, with his love for me and my mother. And yet his hard work made it possible for me to have the financial freedom to find those healing strategies.

After a lifetime of rejecting his heritage, which he and I both mistook for superficial things like his business and his particular style of life, I found his real gift to me, his vision of a better world expressed in words as rough hewn as the oak bowl he had been carving for Lauren the day he died. Now, with the warm water coursing down over me, I saw that if I were to choose to collapse in my weepiness, refusing the pastor's invitation to speak at his funeral, I would be rejecting his most primal gift.

Those waves of energies continued to pulse through me all night keeping me from sleep with a flood of images of men of the Scandinavian forests. These energies were healing me from my alienation from male voices by showing me they were shouting out in a grasp for dominance, but also crudely struggling in frustration to articulate a sense of lost humanity. I saw that my curious impulse twenty-five years earlier to write that abstruse article about Thomas Aquinas in the cool basement at Mount Saint Michael's was the first formal step in a task I had unknowingly been given by these imagined men pushing up inside me. Like Emilie Conrad Da'Oud, I had been driven to find something more basic than everyday reality. While she located it by finding her way through the deceptive vocabularies of primitive dance until she discovered the movement of the cells, I had to work my way through the abstract languages of philosophy and theology, which had usurped such a disproportionate amount of power over other kinds of voices. In that journey, I have had to find out how to put into words the connections between abstract ideas about *body* and *spirit* and the sensual emotional experiences of reality from which they derive their meaning.

The next morning, awake and filled with energy even though I had not slept, I walked to the pulpit at Holy Spirit Church and spoke about my father's rage.

SECTION III

A Map for Pilgrims

How can we work together?
to heal a world that makes little sense,
that makes little of the senses,
that is fast eroding the senses, replacing them with
prosthetic video display terminals and virtual realities?

How can we together become more impelled by a respect
for commonly felt human needs for food, shelter, decent
work and health care over greed, nationalism and religious
sectarianism?

How can we of many faiths, ethnicities, values, and personal preferences forge a healing consensus?

CONSENSUS ORIGINALLY MEANT sensing together. It recalls older ways of interaction where people passed time with each other eating, drumming, chanting, sharing tobacco, often in silence, teasing their raucous spirits out of the ethereal and divisive realms of untethered opinions into the common sense of the fire's heat and the smell of soup. Cut off from those older ways, beset by the turbulence of city life, we have to find our own peculiar ways back from ghostly private and sectarian ideas to a common sense.

Somatics practices, shaped within the experimental democratic atmosphere of the modern West, have their modest contribution to make to the efforts of many people—community organizers, educators, spiritual leaders, psychologists, writers, artists, political activists—who are working to create a more humane world. Shared practices of breathing, feeling, seeing, hearing and moving can make it easier for good-willed people of ideologically conflicting abstract beliefs to collaborate on basic human needs. To engage in these readily available practices requires nothing more arcane than paying attention, speaking directly with each other, opening our hearts and rolling up our sleeves for the hard work ahead.

FOR MANY OF US, the distance between the physicality of everyday life and the world of spiritual vision is vast. We have been born somewhere along a journey initiated by or forced upon parents, grandparents or great-grandparents from an Old World, who were fleeing poverty or war, seeking a better life, or worse, sold into slavery. The widespread disruptions of old communities have left large groups of people wandering in strange lands, where their keepsake rituals and images of things divine seem like museum pieces. Few among us can claim the rootedness enjoyed by the Cochiti Indians or Serbian peasants who have been situated on their lands practicing their rituals for at least two thousand years.

Although we have been thrown into the situation of pilgrims, we have not been prepared with the necessary tools.

IN A LOCAL support group of Cambodian refugees from Pol Pot's persecutions, I listened to a man, whose legs still bore the scars of the large-linked chains that had been wrapped around him for several months, who said this about his situation and that of his family: "We survived the torture by letting our souls leave our bodies; now they are gone and we do not know where they are. Our old healers know how to find them, but they, too, are gone."

Well-meaning physicians at a local hospital had embedded in his leg electrodes whose intermittent shocks were designed to heal scar tissue. The physicians were unaware that electrodes giving off slightly higher charges are routinely used as instruments of torture.

NO MATTER HOW dualistic one's explicit beliefs may be, the pilgrim has to come to terms both with bodily and spiritual realities.

He or she has to cultivate vitality to walk for long periods with enough wind to walk up steep inclines, the resilience to recover quickly from falls and sprains, a sense of balance to negotiate precipitous trails, ingenuity for finding proper nourishment. The pilgrim has to have keen senses to pick out the right openings in the forest, the sound of a distant stream and the smell of a healing herb. More is needed than basic survival skills. One has to familiarize oneself with fear in its first moments of arousal, before it gains enough strength to scare one off the path. If the pilgrimage is to be any more than just another walk, one must have the delicate sensitivity to peristalsis, lymph flow and breath to be ready to accept those graced moments when images begin to flicker up through flesh, calling one into visionary worlds.

In addition to physical fitness, sensibility and flexibility, the pilgrim has to have inspiration. The music and poetry of Afro-Christian spirituality carried generations through their dark night of slavery; sweats, fasts, chants and stories allowed native Americans to survive the virulent efforts by our government to wipe out their rituals and languages. The well-known accounts of survivors of the Nazi camps testify to the essential role of spiritual vision in physical survival. The visionary writings of Dostoevsky, Soloviev and Berdyaev enabled many Russian dissidents to outlast Stalinism.

The pilgrim is different from the missionary. The medieval missionary was convinced that he possessed a truth unknown to the non-believers. Always in the vanguard of colonizing armies, he preached his Trinitarian and sexual dogmas to subjugated— often tortured—people whom he typically considered subhuman. The modernist missionary was secular. Proud of having disabused himself of spiritual dogmatisms by scientism and philosophical relativism, he traveled to the far reaches of the world with his demythologized notions of property rights, chemical pesticides and antibiotics. The souls and soils of many cultures have been depleted, often to the brink of extinction, by four centuries of those two kinds of missionary activities.

Unlike missionaries, pilgrims will evoke hospitality only if they come empty-handed and empty-minded. Settling and resettling in the midst of strange and inhospitable cities requires help from many quarters and from people who have different and often hostile beliefs and who speak unknown languages. Surviving as a pilgrim requires that one be able to show gratitude for kindness along the path, in the recognition that he or she can't make it alone.

Recovering a sense of our reality as pilgrims reminds us that whenever anyone feels that he or she has arrived, it would be best to engage in some serious reflection to diagnose the illusion. "Pilgrimage" reminds us that we still have a lot of work to do. While there is a sense in which the divine is always at hand, there is the paradox that to reach the divine we need to keep on the road to "somewhere else," where our relations with our loved ones will be fuller, our neighborhoods warmer and more contactful, the sick and the dying better cared for, children better educated, air and water less polluted.

The sense of being on a pilgrimage also reminds us that there are ecstasies to be had beyond the delights of the everyday, which help one keep up the long journey of healing.

In these final chapters I show how I have gone about combining and testing these nutrients to create a pilgrim method, which integrates physical and spiritual realities, along with more democratic methods of community governance. The method has three components:

1. Awakening and supporting the unfolding of the embodied spirit of inquiry in the members of the institution, whether that institution be a school, healing center, training institute, community organization, church or family;

2. The restoration of the capacity for detailed story-telling as a method for supporting the unfolding and creative organization of that questioning; and

3. Finding ways to create strategic plans for effective healing strategies, personal and social, which do justice to the density of people's experience.

10

The Spirit of Wonder

The pilgrimage will stall if no one wants to go:
    if people are resigned to their present state;
    if their capacities for following the scent of truth have
been so eviscerated by personal abuse in families, or by
sociopolitical abuse in war, schools and churches that they
don't have energy for the journey;
    if training in physical rigidity and conformity has been
so successful they can't mobilize themselves;
    if they are just too afraid to leave home.

How CAN WE awaken people to value their own underground
currents of passion, which are intense enough to carry them forward
on a lifetime of commitment to learn, investigate, experiment,
document, revise and dare to say what they have discovered? How
evoke that restless longing for meaning and justice which provides
the surprising resources of physical stamina to carry on when one
is exhausted and in despair?

Any responses to those questions must take account of the fact
that wonder is radically physical. You see it in the open eyes and
exploratory movements of the loved infant, starting to make dis-
tinctions among the various elements of her world. You feel it
emerging from the sinking of your heart as you see a homeless

woman and her child on the street in the rain with all their belongings in a shopping cart, and ask "why?" You witness it in the endless vitality of the scientist, who stays in her lab late into the night and on the weekends, hot in pursuit of the solution to a problem that has so far eluded her community of researchers. You feel it in the rush of blood and quivering of limbs when you see an unusual sunset or marvel at the vastness of the night sky or find yourself in the profundity of wondering about the meaning of a loved one's sudden death.

It is precisely its physicality that makes the child's spirit of wonder susceptible to quelling, even to serious abuse. In an earlier book, I told the story of a retired CIA officer, Ivy League-educated, upper-class, urbane, who was unable to respond directly to questions about the simplest sensations: "Do you find that your weight goes through one foot more heavily than another?" "Do you feel the breeze more on one area of your body than another?" To such questions, he would give the strange, seemingly Cartesian reply, "How can one really say?" Puzzled by these responses from an obviously sensitive, intelligent and experienced adult, I pursued those questions until one day we came to the point where he recalled incidents where as an infant his mother had ridiculed him for expressing his liking certain kinds of music that she thought were tasteless. He said that from then on, he was afraid of telling what he experienced.

That same physicality accounts for the effectiveness of Somatic strategies on its awakening. Moshe Feldenkrais made it the foundation for his work. Like Carl Rogers, he argued that the infant, far from being a *tabula rasa*, possesses enormous capacities for learning. He marveled at the infant's rapid acquisition of more complex skills than we will ever have to learn in subsequent periods of our lives: "There was no method, no system in our learning to walk, speak, or count, no examinations, no prescribed term in which to complete the learning, no preset, clearly expressed aim to be attained. This apparently aimless method produces practically no failures of learning in the normally constituted human, and under its conditions we become mature persons, whether well educated or completely illiterate. Formal teachings from childhood to adulthood seem to overlook the fact that there are ways of learning that lead to growth and maturity with practically no failures. Formal teaching is more concerned with 'what' is taught than with 'how'; its failures are very frequent."[43]

The life of wonder is also spiritual. Cultivation of muscles, larynx and joints can easily lead to dead-ends in despair and addiction unless one makes contact with visions of life powerful enough to carry one through the various challenges that will appear along the road. Being seized by this spirit breaks the brittle shell of everyday self-absorption and sweeps us away into the depths of compassion for human pain. It opens our perceptions to the vastness of the cosmos; it renders our hopes receptive to infinite resources of wisdom and love.

I caught on to the importance of the spirit of wonder as a young adult, when I began philosophical studies as a Jesuit-in-training and gained the vague intuition that wonder would guide me out of the brainwashed haze created by my personal and religious history. At the same time, I became puzzled about the radical gulf between the exaltation of the spirit of wonder and its debasement in the institutions I encountered.

Our Jesuit studies paid great attention to Plato's ideal of education, particularly as outlined in *The Republic* and *The Symposium*. His pedagogy was homoerotic, sybaritic, situated within a matrix of sensual pleasure and muscular suppleness. The seeker after wisdom had to be aroused from the slumbers of everyday consciousness by gymnastics, music and the arts. A radically physical eros would lead the way, impelling him beyond a temporary lust for a single beautiful boy to all beautiful bodies to beautiful souls in ugly bodies still further into the region of beautiful institutions and laws, higher to the abstract realms of mathematics and philosophy, climaxing in the orgastic penetration of Beauty Itself.

There was a constant debate within Jesuit philosophy studies about the differences between Plato and Aristotle. Aristotle designed a pedagogy that was peripatetic rather than recumbent. He put the emphasis not so much on the consuming passion to know, but on the the unfolding of the childlike spirit of wonder, a more contemplative kind of human inquiry. Rejecting Plato's hypothetical realm of preexisting Ideals, he argued that all knowledge, no matter how abstract or elevated, has its origins in bodily sensations. As a consequence, an appropriate pedagogy demanded giving attention to the refinement of the student's sensibility.

Through our historical studies, I came to learn that medieval church schools, the proto-universities, were heirs of the Platonic Academy and the Aristotelian Lyceum. But Christian, Kabbalistic, and Muslim mystical intellectuals went a step further than Plato and Aristotle by sacralizing eros and the spirit of wonder. Only within these deep underground currents of human experience, they argued, can a restricted bodily person enjoy intercourse with a transcendent Spirit. To that end, their methods of teaching put even more significance than did the Greeks on cultivating physicality through the practices of breathing, chanting, repetitive movements, and sensory discrimination to which I was introduced in the Jesuit novitiate.

(Later I was to become aware that the old universities of Asia embodied a similar ideal. Intellectual excellence required the refined cultivation of the learner's sensibilities and passions. To this day, even with widespread Westernization, it is not uncommon to meet Asian scholars and scientists who regularly practice qi gong, t'ai chi chu'an, hatha yoga, zazen or vipassana while pursuing their research in particle physics or analytic philosophy. The same is true of the older cultures of Africa, pre-Columbian America and the Arctic Circle, where the gradual acquiring of wisdom depends on a lifetime of cultivating the most refined qualities of sensation and physical stamina.)

With the rise of the New Science in the seventeenth and eighteenth centuries, those widely separated poles on the continuum of experience—the one, muscular and nervous; the other, visionary and cosmic—were moved to the periphery of the Academy. A dispirited region was left at the center: the territory of *reason.* Inquiry, theorizing and writing ceased to be thought of as erotic and wonder-filled stages towards contact with primal aspects of reality. Physical education and the arts were developed as separate disciplines, maintained on the fringes of the Academy to provide a healthy and quietly disciplined container for the evolution of the logical mind. The *body,* now conceived as "the extended thing," an elaborate machine, had to be kept in good condition so a scholar would have both the stamina and the self-control necessary for a life of scholarship. *Spirit* was relegated to a separate, purely intellectual discipline, theology, with practices for its cultivation left to the monasteries. No longer conceived as the result of a natural unfolding of radical inquiry, theology became associated with an overbearing religious dogmatism, a cloistered department in the larger university, where its influence paled as scholars became ever less impressed by theories of divinity uprooted from earth and flesh.

I have spent a good part of my life within communities of intense inquiry and have experienced the scars that come from pitting the physical and spiritual poles of that inquiry against each other.

The medieval climate of the Jesuits was marked by a constant buzz of underground inquiry not unlike that among dissidents in pre-*perestroika* Russia and Middle Europe. Throughout my fourteen years there, small groups of us formed voluntary groups to study forbidden books, contemporary films and novels and non-Christian religions. We engaged in these activities in addition to an already heavy load of work and study and endured the constant harassment of officials. We were driven by a sense that our souls depended on this lifeblood of outside knowledge.

But the practices of everyday Jesuit life, like Communist discipline, were designed to evoke exactly the opposite spirit of obedience, to shape us into the old man's staff.

I found a similar ferment of inquiry in the early Rolfing community. The first Rolfers, uprooted from traditional beliefs and communities, were intent on making sense of things, exploring psychotherapy, meditation practices and a variety of body works.

But despite the fact that such practices awakened deep movements of wonder and flexibility, the theories within the Rolf Institute and other New Age communities became narrowly dogmatic, affirming this or that simplistic notion of human development.

In both worlds, I found only a halfhearted value placed on the spirit of inquiry. In the Jesuit world, known for its intellectual expansiveness, one was constantly reminded of the outer limits of unquestionable papal dogma. In the Rolf Institute, the Line and the Template marked the boundaries of orthodoxy.

It is that strange limit that I have always found imposed on inquiry that eventually prompted me to make the link between *body, spirit,* and democracy. Earlier I cited this quote from the prophet Jeremiah, which Jesus used to explain his own mission, and to which many Christian political thinkers, including contemporary liberation theologians, have turned to justify their spiritual populism:

> I will place my law within them, and write it upon their hearts.... No longer will they have need to teach their friends and kinsmen how to know the Lord. All, from least to greatest, shall know me (*Jer.* 31.33).

If the Holy Spirit is poured into the hearts of all people of good will, no one has the right to dictate truth to the other; the authority to construct worldly versions of truth lies in the people, not as the fragmented atoms of Thomas Hobbes's Leviathan, but as an inspirited collective. Truth was not the exclusive possession of priests or priestesses encountered in secret rites by intuitive visions inaccessible to anyone outside the sanctuary, requiring only humble obedience. It was to be gained bit by bit in dialogue where people challenged each other and built on each other's insights, a model which inspired William James and John Dewey's modern linking of shared experiential inquiry with the construction of a democratic society.

A vigorous, often violent theme of spiritual populism provided a steady counterpoint to the dominant motif of Roman authoritarianism. It first surfaced in the community of Marcion, who was declared a heretic in the second century for rejecting papal and episcopal authority based on the biblical teaching that the divine spirit lives within the hearts of every decent human being. It spread throughout Europe during the high Middle Ages with the preaching of the anarchistic followers of Saint Francis of Assisi. John of Salisbury, Marsilius of Padua and Giambattista Vico refined that teaching into the earliest versions of democractic political theory, which eventually influenced the populism of Luther, Karl Marx and the liberation theologians. John Courteney Murray, the old Jesuit theologian who had introduced me to LSD, followed that line of reasoning in his arguments for the superiority of democracy over monarchy as a home for genuine spirituality.

That ideal was constantly under attack by religious arguments against the trustworthiness of perceptions unmediated by church authority and by secular arguments about the aberrant character of consensual experience. Nowhere did I find communities of people fully willing to organize themselves around the notion that authority abided in a shared spirit of wonder and inquiry.

THE CURRENT OF human experience I am describing runs so deep and is so idiosyncratic in form that it can't be reached by steps laid out by someone else. Each of us has to find our own pathways into it; and by sharing life stories, we can shape our own path.

The effectiveness of the vast network of Twelve Step programs is a testimony to the significance of people telling their own stories and hearing others'. Addicts recovering from lifetimes of pain have found that theories and exhortations only exacerbate their isolation and frustration. In the communal sharing of life stories, people can locate within themselves healing resources more powerful than the forces of self-destruction.

In my case, I have been able to nurture the flicker of that spirit and allow it to expand first by learning through books of the lives of saintly and scientific inquirers, then by getting to know such people: paying close attention to how they have kept alive a deep sense of excitement about unknowns in the midst of a technological and economic barrage of superficial pseudo-answers. Each of us needs to find out how to do the work we were meant to do in our peculiar way, locating our own impulses towards the True, Good and Beautiful. If we can find sources to nurture those impulses, we can also discover what has dampened them and find friends who will be of genuine help on our path.

It was in that context that I became inspired by the work and life of Charlotte Selver.

CHARLOTTE SELVER WAS born in 1901 in a small German town at the confluence of the Ruhr and the Rhine. Half Jewish, she grew up as something of a stubborn misfit, "clumsy and stiff," she says. As a young girl, she resisted her parents' plans for her to become a cultivated woman, marry and raise a family. First, she wanted to be a musician. When her parents thwarted that, she became interested in photography. They also forbade her to do that until one day when she was twelve, she threatened to jump from a nearby bridge! In those early years, she says she found herself troubled by the impoverished state of the steel workers and coal miners of the Ruhr. A young poet awakened that concern, prompting her to make regular forays into the working-class neighborhood of her town in disobedience to her parents' rules.[44]

By eighteen, she was in Munich starting a career as a professional photographer. To her dismay, she found herself serving the vanity of society woman, "primped with curls all over them," instead of carrying out the sensitive artistic explorations which she originally had in mind. She decided to turn to nature photography, and applied for a job as a photographer at a German-Austrian alpine organization. The men in charge turned her down, saying that the job would be too dangerous for a woman.

As she was becoming increasingly frustrated by her attempts to shape her life as an artist, her cousin, a member of Mary Wigman's dance troupe, took her to one of Wigman's original performances. Charlotte became aware of feeling stiff and heavy with bad posture. Her cousin said, "Why don't you do something for yourself?"[44] She turned to studies within the Gymnastik movement, a forerunner of Somatics.

THE DETAILS OF that movement are important. The tendency to forget its largely non-literary lineage, as in the case of women's history, plays into the dominant tendency of our culture to belittle the significance of bodily processes in the evolution of our common wisdom.

An early pioneer of the Gymnastik movement was François Delsarte, born in 1811, a Parisian actor and director of a school of drama. Under the pressure of his job teaching actors, he became fascinated with how certain movements could be expressive and others unexpressive. He gradually developed a method which emphasized the relationship between movement and breathing. He was such a failure in Paris that he decided to emigrate to New York around 1860, where he soon gained a number of students, including Steele McKay and Genevieve Stebbins. In the last years of his life, Delsarte returned to Paris where he died in 1871, forgotten and alone.[45] Stebbins, meanwhile had managed to gain such wide acceptance for the work that two German women, Hede Kallmeyer and Bess Mensendieck heard about it, came to New York to study with her, and took the work back to Germany, where they developed their own systems. Mensendieck's work once again crossed the Atlantic and eventually became the basis for the widely influential posture training method used in East coast prep schools and private universities.

Another pioneer in the Gymnastik movement was the Austrian Leo Kofler. He emigrated to Kentucky in 1877, where he worked as organist and choirmaster until he eventually gained a position at

Saint Paul's Chapel, Trinity Parish, in Manhattan. He and several members of his family had been afflicted by tuberculosis, which in his case affected his larynx. He consulted the throat specialist, Dr. Withfield Ward, who inspired him to immerse himself in studies of the anatomy and physiology of the larynx, the voice and respiration. Out of those studies he healed himself and developed a system for exploring the relationships between what he identified as "natural" breathing and voice, which he described in his *The Art of Breathing*, translated into German in 1897 by Clara Schlaffhorst and Hedwig Andersen, who used it as the inspiration for their Rotenburger School.[46] That translation has persisted through thirty-six editions, and the School still flourishes in Germany. Significant for what it indicates about American intellectual interest in this kind of serious bodily exploration, is the fact that the book rapidly passed out of print in English.

Another pioneer was Emile Jacques-Dalcroze, a musician who lived in Geneva and developed a method of education based on combining rhythmic movements with music. In his Hellerau School, he counted among his students Rudolf von Laban and Mary Wigman who were among the principal creators of movement therapy and modern dance. It was his method which Charlotte first studied. She went to one of the most well-known teachers of that lineage, Rudolf Bode, who taught a form called *Ausdrucksgymnastik*, in which people improvised dance-like exercises to the accompaniment of various musical instruments. She reports that in the midst of one of her classes with him, he suddenly stopped and shouted at her: "There are so many beautiful professions in the world; why did you choose this? You are completely ungifted!" Despite his constant criticism, she persisted in the training and gained certification to teach. At graduation, after doling out praise to each of her classmates about how well his work had been assimilated, he said to her: "You will make your way: you can talk and you can play the piano."

Beginning her professional practice as a teacher of Gymnastik, she was able to succeed with her students by applying her considerable background in improvisational music—she was a member of an orchestra—despite her distaste for the prevalent imitative style within Gymnastik. "I brought [my students] to a high which I was convinced would change their lives. However, when I met them on the street or in company there was not much to see of what we had been sharing during the sessions. Eventually, I had the feeling that the power of music was somehow bringing them into more mobility and made things very much easier for them. I felt that there must be some way to go about liberating oneself in which one doesn't need music."[47]

Then an event took place that would determine the future course of her work. In the early 1920s, tens of thousands of European youth who were participating in the Gymnastik movement gathered at Hellerau, the location of Jacques-Dalcroze's school near Dresden, for a Woodstock-like event where they engaged in group rituals, exercises and discussions of philosophy and politics. (During the early 1930s, this event would be followed up by the fanatical gatherings of the Hitler and Communist Youth Movements.) At this gathering, Charlotte met a woman who had founded the first experimental school in Germany for children orphaned by the war, who told Charlotte about a teacher in Berlin named Elsa Gindler: "She has done wonders for me." Two years later when Charlotte happened to be visiting Berlin, she looked up Gindler's name in the telephone directory, went to her studio, and sat quietly in the corner observing the class in session, "with Elsa's back to me." She says: "In that hour I had the feeling that whatever I had learned was nothing compared with what I felt she offered. Her approach was entirely different. She didn't teach anything!"[48]

Gindler was having the students work on jumping, an activity which Charlotte says was the most horrible thing for her. "I would be like a piece of ice. I was too afraid to even jump over a rope...." In the many accounts Charlotte has related about that class, which was the major turning point in her life, she says virtually nothing about her experiences of sensing or changes in her body affected during the jumping. Instead, she emphasizes Gindler's questions; those caught her attention in a totally new way: "Do you feel what is under your feet? Do you feel the air that you are jumping through? How would it help little Mary when the teacher tells her 'look at Elsie, how beautifully she jumps, do it the same way!' How does it help her?"

Charlotte, who was having such trouble jumping, was suddenly stopped in her tracks when Gindler turned to her and asked: "Do you really want to jump?"[49] Moving to the music of Elsa's questions made Charlotte aware that her previous difficulties in being a graceful student had nothing to do with intrinsic clumsiness on her part, but with her tenacious unwillingness to imitate. Now, by contrast to Gindler, she realized that teachers like Bode who prided themselves on teaching improvisation were making subtle demands on students to make movements like their own.

Charlotte was so inspired by that first class that she approached Gindler, asking to be accepted as her student, only to meet reluctance. Gindler told her to continue her own work, seeing how limited Charlotte had been by the subtle formalisms in Bode's style. Three months later, she returned, again to meet rejection. When Charlotte asked her why, Gindler said that Charlotte had to unlearn everything that she learned and come back to her own nature before Gindler could take responsibility for being her teacher; "that is the most difficult thing to do." Finally, on the third attempt, Gindler accepted her as a student, but not without misgivings. Gindler told her in later years that she had asked herself, "What can I do with this beautiful mannequin?"[50] Charlotte says that she wondered why Gindler never looked at her during the first year of classes. Many years later, she realized that Gindler couldn't stand her. (In listening to Charlotte over the years, I have been struck by how many stories she tells of having been treated by teachers she loved in what, to me, is a very abusive way. But she never speaks of their behavior as anything but ordinary. Perhaps a testimony to what Alice Miller calls the "poisonous pedagogy," which was prevalent in pre-war Europe.)

Finally, one day when they were moving through the studio, Gindler said to her, "Ah, at last, the first movement!" Charlotte says that she nearly fainted.

The uniqueness of Gindler's work consisted in direct basic questions about experience where students were encouraged to engage in their own discoveries without preconceived answers or formulaic recipes. She did not even give her work a name. Charlotte says she once called it simply *Arbeit am Menschen*, "work with humans," and also *Nachentfaltung*, "after-unfolding" or "unfolding at a later stage of one's life." The method originated from Gindler's experiences of healing herself from tuberculosis which she contracted during the great flu epidemic of 1918. Her physician told her that a lobe of her lungs was critically diseased and recommended that she go to a sanatorium in the Alps—to die, Gindler assumed. As a young teacher from a working-class family, she couldn't even entertain the possibility of undertaking such an expensive attempt at a cure, which she thought would be futile even if she could afford it. As for what happens next, Charlotte repeatedly tells the primary healing story this way (I suspect something else happened as well): Gindler says that she decided to clean herself, inside and out, and to stay quiet. She hoped that if she were able to activate other lobes of the lungs so as to allow the diseased lung to rest, a healing process might occur. Each day, for more than a year she spent time patiently attending to her breath trying to rest the diseased portion of her lungs. She fully recovered her health, in the course of which she recognized the enormous healing potential in simple awareness of the functioning of the organism.

Charlotte, perhaps with Gindler's original encouragement, insists that this healing came out of nowhere as a completely new idea: the same kind of claim was attributed to the Rolf Template and Recipe. Such a version overlooks the fact that Gindler had spent over a decade practicing Gymnastik methods, including some which concerned breathing. In my view, it seems more accurate to assume that she applied to her own concerns what she had learned from her training as a teacher of Gymnastik in the Rotenburger School. Instead of slavishly imitating ready-made techniques, she took only the core inspiration of their more complicated methods, on the intuition that quiet and simplicity would reveal new capacities for healing. Her genius was not in creating something out of nothing, but, like Ida Rolf, in being sufficiently inventive to use in a new way the materials that were available to her and having the courage to apply them until she found out how to make them work to save her life.

Her success in healing herself led Gindler to a radical simplification of the methods of Gymnastik which she had previously learned. "She was fired with the recognition that to learn to sense one's own functioning, and, beyond that, to sense and allow changes in the attitudes accompanying it, was not only possible, but could in fact become an approach to living entirely different from learning methods and practices handed down by others. What had at first been an intuitive therapeutic attempt became a *Weltanschauung* far beyond any bounds of therapy."[51]

Charlotte speaks often of Gindler's social concerns; like the words of the young poet writing about the working-class, those concerns have permeated Charlotte's teaching, causing her continually to stimulate her students to reflect on how the sensing work is related to the serious problems of the world: "The greatest influence on me was the way Elsa Gindler lived. She was there for everybody. She was so conscious of the influence which poverty and oppression had on so many people. The way she went through the Hitler time: working, hiding people who were persecuted, sharing her very meager rations with them, helping them to get out of the country, even at the risk of her own life, all this has been working in me."[52] "I am still her student," she said to me recently, her eyes wide with devotion.

Despite Gindler's severe criticism, Charlotte persevered in studying with her until she gained authorization to teach the work herself. When Hitler came to power in 1933, she was teaching at the University of Leipzig. She reports that the widespread interest in cultivating the body which characterized the youth movements—

love for the natural environment, nudity, health, self-expression—degenerated into the *Kraft durch Freude* ("strength through joy") fanaticism of the Hitler youth. Professors at the university were asked to wear the swastika. "We were so surrounded by spies that the only safe place was in a private auto," she says, but even there people were often stopped, asked for papers and arrested. She tells of memories of arriving for classes at Gindler's Berlin studio trembling in fear from what she saw along the drive from Leipzig. She describes the dramatic contrast between the increasingly violent world outside obsessed with ideology and the quiet of the studio where people were engaged in an inquiry into sensing.

After five years of putting up with this terror, Charlotte emigrated to New York. Arriving there with only five dollars, she had to set to work immediately as a companion for an older woman. During her few free hours, she earned extra money by doing massage. Little by little, she began to give sessions of her own work shaped by her studies with Gindler. Her first break occurred when one of her students introduced Charlotte to her friend, Erich Fromm. Charlotte says that after their meeting, she returned home and told her mother: "I have met my brother today." Fromm was so impressed by her work that he encouraged his fellow psychoanalysts at the William Alanson White Association to study with her. With that support, she was able to begin giving herself completely to developing her Gindler-inspired methods of work. Fritz Perls became her student, and his version of Gestalt Therapy reflects the impact of her work without acknowledgment.

At one point, one of her students said to her that Charlotte's teaching was a form of Zen, and brought her a translation of a book by a French priest, Hubert Benoit. Charlotte was amazed by the similarities of that philosophy to her own experiences. Her aunt sent her Alan Watts's *The Spirit of Zen*, which so impressed her that she looked him up when she visited California in the early 1960s. Strongly touched by her work, he once exclaimed: "This is the living Zen." He introduced her to the San Francisco Zen Buddhist community recently founded by Suzuki Roshi, with whom she developed a friendship. He invited her to become a regular teacher of Zen students. To this day, that community is important in her life.

A crucial difference exists between her work and the popular image of it as a form of Zen. One day, during a seminar at the Zen Center's Green Gulch Farm, she said to me that people mistakenly equate her work with Zen. "Zen masters have something to teach;" she said, with an edge of impish humor, "I only explore."

Her approach is more accurately described as practical phenomenology in the tradition of Edmund Husserl, than as a Western Zen. It is an inquiry into experience simply as it is given, without interpretation or any conclusions about the value or "reality" of any particular experience.[53] Despite its claims for being empty and formless, Zen is a tightly structured world, both verbally and nonverbally: one sits, walks, chants and eats in prescribed ways. The tradition includes volumes of interpretative literature about the status of different kinds of experiences. As in other ecclesiastical groups, Zen has ordained teachers authorized to dictate standards of practice. Charlotte's work challenges students to question any authoritative judgment ranging from postures for sitting, to social policies governing health care for infants. Her work embodies an experimental spirit that when cultivated can lead to a community's recovery of their common sensibilities.

Her late husband, Charles Brooks, pinpoints that unique quality of Charlotte's populist spirit in describing its impact on him: "During my life, I have often rejected one authority only to accept another. Underneath, I was afraid at the thought of living in a world where there was not Someone, somewhat like myself, who knew. But I have now come to feel that to know what one is doing with life, it is no use to consult authorities. It is precisely through the veils which authorities have spun for us that our own ears and eyes and nerves must begin to penetrate if our hands are to grasp the world and our hearts to feel it. We must recover our own capacity to taste for ourselves. Then we shall be able to judge also."[54]

C HARLOTTE'S WORK COULD not be simpler. In a typical class, she invites people to investigate sitting and standing. During a period of two hours, people sit—in whatever way they happen to sit—and stand —in whatever way they happen to end up on their feet. The only goal is to become increasingly more awake to the many aspects revealed by experiences of sitting, coming to standing, standing and coming back to sitting. There is no judgment or theory about the "right" way to do it; the point is to coax one's interest away from habitual obsessions to the immediate sensations of a particular activity as it unfolds. She typically raises a few questions about the activity, which never seem prepared or repetitive but arise out of a genuine curiosity about what catches her attention to our activity: "Is your breathing there for your standing?" "Are you there for the floor?"

She does not only work with so-called "body movement" exercises (she often gets furious when people apply to what she does the words "body" or "body work," retorting that she is interested in humans). She asks people to notice what happens if they hear the sound of a gong or taste a grape or lift a small rock. "The basis of our work is that when one gradually begins to go into each activity anew, one loses one's habitual stance. And this approaching each activity anew means a person who is awake and changeable. With all this comes movability and elasticity. So that one does not always toot into the old horn."[55]

In a class one evening, Charlotte invited a small group of us to walk very slowly around the room, paying particular attention to the contact between the soles of our feet and the rush mats on the hardwood floor. I was elsewhere, floating among worries about conflicts from the day's work, my impending divorce, and my stiff neck. Drifting through the room with my attention on that "elsewhere," I suddenly woke up to the sole of my right foot brushing the mats underneath, the solidity of the floor supporting me, the sounds of others, the feel of the air, and Charlotte's voice saying, "ah, at last, you are there for your feet." Her ability to notice that precise moment when my attention shifted from my self-involved chatter into the experience of my foot gave me a sense of how I could more easily inhabit my muscles and bones and become less preoccupied with internal conversations.

The work involves far more than sensing. Like many of her fellow refugees from pre-War Europe, she has a keen nose for fanaticism in its most subtle forms. She is deeply concerned about the degradation of the sensible world and the human community. She feels that Gindler taught her the intimate connection between sensory awakening and larger human questions: "When I started to study with Elsa Gindler, I was very deeply impressed by her including the whole cosmos in her work. She made us conscious of the fact that every person has his potentials, and how very important it is that we make it possible that more and more people can develop these potentials."[56]

Charlotte was the first person to give workshops at Esalen Institute, and it was indirectly through that connection that I came upon her work in 1967, nearly twenty years before I actually took a class with her. Another Jesuit and I went to a workshop given in a Presbyterian church in Palo Alto by an early student of hers, Bernie Gunther, who had just published (to Charlotte's outrage) a best-seller called *Sensory Awareness: Below Your Mind,* a large, glossy paperback filled with photographs of young naked bodies on the Esalen lawns and in the baths touching each other all over with blissful looks in their eyes, lifting little rocks, feeling the grass, feeding each other pieces of banana. Bernie, a converted gym teacher from the Midwest, gave rambling lectures about how Charlotte's work incarnated the ideas of Teilhard de Chardin, Norman O. Brown, John of the Cross, Sri Aurobino, Darwin and Freud: all precursors of a new state of consciousness in which we would all become one polymorphously perverse body in a state of continual orgasm, with no authoritarian leaders ordering us to put the plug on our excitement. Despite his untutored erotic mysticism and the weirdness of trying to feel my feet on a cold floor and the embarrassment of having to put my hands on other people in the class, I was affected by his words. I was just becoming aware of how physically brittle and out of touch I felt.

As I became involved with the more dramatic bioenergetics and Rolfing practices, I forgot Charlotte's simple work until towards the end of my doctoral studies at Yale in 1970, just before beginning my Rolf training. Elissa registered to take a series of classes with Charlotte in New York on the same days that she was being Rolfed by Ida's son. She would return to New Haven from those classes and tell me in great detail what had happened—what Charlotte said, even how she looked, and what the students did. With a background in modern dance and music not unlike Charlotte's pre-Gindler education, Elissa was deeply affected by Charlotte's radical invitation to find her own movement and perceptions. Although she had long considered herself to be a rebel, Elissa was awakened by Charlotte's fresh questions to realize how conformist she had become. She had managed to find a way to imitate her teachers in place of finding her own movement, even though her teachers were outstanding innovators like Hanya Holm, José Limon and Martha Graham. What Elissa said about those classes, and how she described Charlotte seemed to penetrate the very mind of my cells. It affected my way of working with myself and my ideas about working with other people.

When I eventually met her and took a class from her in 1982, it was like the first time I visited Rome, where I had the uncanny experience that I already knew the territory, having for so long read the Latin classics, lives of the saints and church history. By then, I had become familiar with simple sensing work, having purged my early meditation practices of their theological trappings. But I found something unexpected in her curious questions: "When you come to standing, are you there for the air around you?" "Does the floor support you?" "Is your hand there for your partner's shoulder?"

Although both Charlotte and her students have emphasized

sensing as the unique focus of her work, I believe that is not what distinguishes her work from others in the field; it is her genius at evoking the numbed spirit of wonder with the continually fresh question. Many teachers in the Somatics field, and many meditation teachers, emphasize turning attention towards sensation. But their work, filled with many preconceived answers and strategies, does not approach the radical quality of Charlotte's open inquiry.

She recently summed up her work in words that accurately link *body, spirit,* and democracy: "How is it that we can help people to become more awake, and how, after they begin to wake up, they learn to trust their own sensations. And how it is that they can discover that they really can see, and hear, and sense; and that this alone can be a very powerful agent in one's life. One can learn not to restrict one's view; to feel oneself as a member of this planet we all live on. It's important that people learn to stop circling around themselves and instead to become open to the world and active."[57]

At ninety-two, despite many injuries during the past years from falls and auto accidents, severe deafness and her husband Charles's death in 1991, Charlotte is still moving around vigorously. In addition to teaching virtually all the time, she takes regular walks, loves to dance and play. She continues her yearly teaching trips to Guadalajara, Zurich, Maine, Southern California and Japan.

WHAT DOES THIS radically simple, primordial awakening of sensations have to do with spirituality? Charlotte herself comments on that question: "What people call 'mystic'—the experiences one has, for instance in breathing, in balance, or whatever it is, in contact with another person—this can be very clearly experienced and yet experienced as a wonder, too. In other words, I feel it would be marvelous if one could work to pinpoint certain very clear revelations, which come out of experience and which in themselves are astonishing. The revelations can come from the very smallest experience. For instance, eating."[58]

Life Stories and Abstract Theories

There is a story which I have used before and shall use again:
A man wanted to know about mind, not in nature, but in
his private large computer. He asked it (no doubt in his best
Fortran), "Do you compute that you will ever think like a
human being?" The machine then set to work to analyze its
own computational habits. Finally, the machine printed its
answer on a piece of paper, as such machines do. The man
ran to get the answer and found, neatly typed, the words:
THAT REMINDS ME OF A STORY.[59]

M Y PATH OUT of the brainwashing miasma of my upbringing
has wound along parallel ridges. One consists of delving into the
realities revealed in breathing, peristalsis, touching and muscu-
loskeletal rigidities; the other, in sniffing out the details of the lives
of creative people—saints, Somatics innovators, philosophers,
kind men and women. I have needed to shift back and forth
between both trails so as to gain a sense of the world that is reliable
and sane. I found that bare experience and passionate inquiry are
not enough. We have to be able to speak with one another about
how to move ahead and develop appropriate strategies for living
more humanely.

In older cultures, story-telling was the next step in moving from puzzle towards practical answers. Christian, Sufi, Buddhist and Hindu monastic orders place a study of stories from the lives of their saints on a par with meditation in their daily spiritual practices. Stories are at the center of native American, African and Pacific Islander wisdom traditions.

In our own story-deprived culture, it is significant that Twelve Step programs have been so successful and have expanded beyond alcohol and drug addictions to virtually every human problem. That is not because every problem is accurately described as an addiction, but because the oldest and most important form of healing comes from feeling connected to a community knit together by stories told in ruthlessly honest detail. When a community or a family loses their practices of story-telling, the basic web of interconnection is rent.

Our capacity for story-telling has been severely traumatized. Dislocations of peoples have destroyed the passing on of old stories. A modernist intellectual and technological climate denigrates the truth value of stories. The language of schools—of the thirteenth century Cathedral School of Notre Dame to the University of California—disembodies the spirit of human inquiry. Both the fleshy muck of ordinary life and colorful visionary passion have been excised in deference to the banal canons of the APA and *Chicago Manuals of Style*. (New disciplines are indeed featuring stories. Feminist theory, ethnic studies and peace and conflict studies include a great deal of story-telling, even though the acceptable language is typically highly abstract and filled with technical jargon. Students clearly want stories and help create interdisciplinary majors that reward story-making. But the success of these tentative endeavors remains in question, assaulted by conservative intellectual critics and endangered by scarce economic resources.)

In the first chapter, I introduced the notion that because abstract theories about reality originated in actual life stories of individuals or communities who lived or traveled through particular geographies, the abstractions bear the traces of those journeys. As the genetic story recedes in time, the abstraction tends to remain as if it were a Platonic Ideal, eternally present in the mind of an absolute being. In that uprootedness from the original struggles and dreams, the abstraction takes on the air of being a universal norm for judging the validity of other stories. Later devotees of that viewpoint, deprived of details of the halting personal journey towards a particular theory, are left feeling inferior to the sainted founders, fated to be disciples resuscitated by someone else's inspiration.

Unearthing the fossil tracks of the pilgrimages of saints and innovators reveals that they are not all that different from the rest of us: they are puzzled, angry, selfish, wanting to love, somewhat intelligent and resourceful, and they managed to find a way to a healing viewpoint. Getting close to the wayward contours of their lives passes on a spark which can give us the sustenance we need to face our own hurdles. I have described what I have learned from the paths of Ignatius Loyola, Ida Rolf, Emilie Conrad Da'Oud, Charlotte Selver, and Bonnie Bainbridge Cohen (in the next chapter), comparing the precise details of their lives with the architectural elements of their formal ideas. It is impossible to grasp the meaning of their ideas without understanding the details of their lives.

❀

I HAD AN early intuition about the importance of stories when I was only twelve years old and read a biography of Saint Francis of Assisi. More than any catechetical teaching, his story made me want to follow a path of love and freedom from material encumbrances. I was to discover that not all lives of the saints were equally inspiring. The more common are devout hagiographies, which appear in every religious tradition, written by disciples with the aim of portraying the saint as a unique being whose visions and commitment to goodness were so compelling that he or she was never interested in food, sex, money, being praised or having fun like the rest of us. I had to read scores of them as a young Jesuit. They depicted saints as so far different from me that reading about them depressed me by giving me the feeling I could never reach such an exalted state.

I found encouragement from a second literary genre which follows the canons of historical research, where the writer tries to ferret out exact details of the saint's life, the seedy as well as the so-called uplifting. The Jesuit James Broderick, who chronicled the lives of major Jesuit saints, was an example. His account of Aloysius Gonzaga, for example, based on years of searching through records of sixteenth century Italy, peeled away the angelic pink tones that covered the surface of his popular image, to reveal him as another brash, sex-driven adolescent son of the Mantuan aristocracy, like today's young bucks who cruise the streets of Arezzo and Todi on their Vespas. Those very details made his saintliness stand out all the more. He allowed himself to be deeply moved by the sick peasants dying in the streets of Ravenna and Rome. He had the courage to stand apart from his adolescent friends and divert his Latin passions into a life of service, moving away from his destined path towards becoming a feudal warlord or an ecclesiastical prince.

The ambiguity of Broderick's accounts of sanctity are reflected in the films *The Mission, Blackrobe,* and *At Play in the Fields of the Lord,* all of whom have characters inspired by Jesuits detailed in Broderick's research. For example, his major study of Isaac Jogues, Jean de Brebeauf and companions, *The North American Martyrs,* paints the dark picture portrayed in Brian Moore's *Black Robe.* In contrast to the pious myth of pure-hearted men selflessly bringing the saving message of Christ to the savages, Broderick pieced together the lives that actually emerged from the details of the monthly letters which they had to write to their Roman superiors. They are afraid and self-involved; they wonder why they are interfering with the lives of these strange peoples, whom they both love and look down upon; they argue with each other; they are cynical about the worldly aims of their fellow French soldiers and traders. They do not approach their final apocalypse, where the Iroquois would devour their hearts, joyfully singing like the early

Christians marching into the Coliseum to be torn apart by the lions. They are afraid. And yet, like Rembrandt's painting of the Holy Family, whose thickly applied black pigments serve to make the small fragments of light even more radiant, Broderick's ruthlessly honest portrait lets the meaning of their lives and their executions shine out more powerfully than any pious account. You say, moved to tears, that there is something truly human here.

As a young Jesuit philosopher, I gained a rare glimpse into the soul of medieval theology when I happened across a brief but carefully detailed biography of Thomas Aquinas, which challenged his popular image of being an antiseptic rationalist Christian, sure of his way towards a logically encapsulated First Mover. Its author Josef Piper called it, *The Silence of St. Thomas,* from a crucial moment late in Aquinas's life which Church theologians have glossed over. Two years before he died, at the end of a private mass he turned to his secretary and said that the visions he had just received made his writings seem like straw. He did not write another word during the two years between then and his death, leaving incomplete his major work, the *Summa Theologiae.*

Piper's biography highlights the traces left by Aquinas's ambivalences in the deceptive medieval scholastic form, which, like contemporary academic form, belies the hurly-burly of inquiry. His theorizing was driven by not uncommon uncertainties. He was besieged by such intense sexual lusts that he came close to having intercourse with a voluptuous woman visiting his family home on the eve of his entry into the cloister. He often felt disgust for the mediocrity of friars in his Dominican community. He was enraptured by the empiricist philosophy described in texts of Aristotle, which were reintroduced into Europe for the first time in eight centuries by Islamic theologians when he was just embarking on his studies of theology. Rejecting the idealism of Plato and embracing Aristotle's biologically-inspired holistic philosophy, he had serious doubts about the eternal existence of a separate soul, doubts that were obvious enough to earn him condemnation as a heretic by the theological faculties of Cambridge and Paris shortly after he died. Those facts were conveniently repressed two hundred years later when he was enshrined as the official theologian of the anti-Protestant Church.

Father Healy did not allow us to read Broderick, Piper and similarly accurate chroniclers. Those books were locked behind a steel grate in the special section of the library along with the works of such dangerous thinkers as Teilhard de Chardin, Gabriel Marcel and Rollo May, which could be withdrawn only with written permission from him, which was rarely given.

Pious hagiography is by no means an exclusive possession of the Christian West. You find sanitized lives of saints among all the more conceptually-oriented religions whose self-righteous piety stands in contrast with the bawdiness of Yiddish, African, Middle Eastern and native American stories that delight in telling about the foibles of their wise men and women.

CAROLINE WALKER BYNUM, a historian whose work has focused on the role of the body in medieval Christian mysticism, contrasts tragic and comic modes of writing history:

> If tragedy tells a cogent story, with a moral and a hero, and undergirds our sense of the nobility of humanity, comedy tells many stories, achieves a conclusion only by coincidence and wild improbability, and undergirds our sense of human limitation, even our cynicism about our motives and self-awareness.... the comic is not necessarily the pleasant, or at least it is the pleasant snatched from the horrible by artifice and with acute self-consciousness and humility ... a comic stance welcomes voices hitherto left outside, not to absorb or mute them but to allow them to object and contradict. Its goal is the pluralistic, not the total. It embraces the partial as partial.[60]

The comic mode interrupts the relentless onrush of male vociferousness, including my own, leaving room for silence and the emergence of new, previously mute voices, fresh ideas and images.

❀

I FOUND HAGIOGRAPHICAL whitewashing also in Somatics. The pioneers are presented in a such way so that you never imagine them going to the toilet, having miserable sexual experiences, flirting with Nazism, staying awake nights wondering if they know anything at all, because they have caused a client more rather than less pain. The effects of that kind of censored story-telling are as disempowering for their students as the devout tales of haloed saints because they portray a breed of human being out of the modest reach of most of us, with super-human powers of perception and touch.

But if, like Father Broderick, you ferret out the details of the lives of these people, you find that we are all moving in the same world with the same modest, yet adequate, equipment. What looms as unique in Ida Rolf's life, for example, is not her Recipe, her ordinary intelligence nor her modicum of human compassion, but her dogged determination to follow out her intuition that gravity is of enormous importance in the life of spirit, and paying careful attention to the results of using her hands on other people to follow up that intuition. Those details are not easy to come by. She didn't try to hide them, often telling stories of how she developed her work. But those stories were not given the kind of theoretical weight and priority accorded the Recipe and the Template. In retrospect, I realize how much I missed in my years of study with Ida by being so pressured to focus on those detached ideas. Trying so hard to implement the details of the Recipe and see deviations from the Template, I did not fully profit from the opportunities I had for an intimate contact with her hard-earned wisdom about precise sensitivity and courageous experimentalism. For students who never knew her, those abstractions appeared to be finished products, not shaped roughly from a lifetime of kneading

195

the folds of human flesh. And significantly, when she wrote her only book, she tells none of the stories that led to the abstractions. You can find such narratives only in the books published by her assistant Rosemary Feitis and myself.

❦

I HAVE EXPERIMENTED with how story-telling can impact the shape of institutions in two realms: academic and religious.

Story-telling is the heart of our thirteen-year-old graduate program in Somatics Psychology. Our curriculum is based on historical studies of many of the pioneers of Somatics, giving students a sense of how these people went about their discoveries in very human and comprehensible ways. Over a two- or three-year period, students are encouraged to detail the key stories of their own life histories and to learn how to help others do the same. Their research papers are to be grounded on traumatic events in their history and in the stories of clients in their internships, which require them to inquire into reliable healing methods, after the pattern of Gindler, Reich and Rolf. Our faculty helps students discover how those life stories are manifested both in their images of their bodies, as well as in their body structures and in the patterns of their emotional lives. We ask each of the students to keep an extensive journal throughout the course of his or her studies entitled: "Towards a Somatics Theory and Practice." In it, they keep records of dreams, memory fragments, collages of drawings and pictures, jottings about meaningful theories. By their final year in the program they are asked to shape this material into an account of how they intend to go about their healing work in the world.

I have also used story-telling methods working with groups of people with different religious commitments. I have asked them to tell stories of how they came to the present shaping of their spiritual vision: events in which they experienced a coming together of bodily experience and spiritual vision, times of healing, intense joy, the death of a loved one, an intense realization in the wilds.

As one tells the details of his or her story, often using drawings and movements to express elements of one's life where words fail, the heavy divisive ideologies of religion typically give way in these groups to the liquid and spacious feelings of compassion, sadness, joy and freedom.

I know that others have used these methods for political organizations and for the reorganization of businesses.

Story is the linguistic form closest to bone and to cosmic vision. It awakens people to the spirit that cannot be caught in logical phrases; it moves people in pain to keep on going; its ironies and unsolved mysteries evoke a sense of our shared humanity, that no one of us can claim to define truth for others.

Getting the details of a story just right is like doing a breathing awareness exercise, or vipassana meditation: it draws attention away from the hypnosis of preconceived ideas into the specific density of life where we share the same air, and the same kinds of human struggles. In that humid and fertile thicket, we might find unsuspected ways to cooperate.

Body-Spirit Maps

At Blackwater Pond

You know how it feels,
wanting to walk into
the rain and disappear—
wanting to feel your life
brighten and grow weightless
as a leaf in the fall.
And sometimes, for a moment,
you feel it beginning—the sense
of escape sharp as knife-blade
hangs over the dark field
of your body, and your soul
waits just under the skin
to leap away over the water.
But the blade,
at the last minute, hesitates
and does not fall,
and the body does not open,
and you are what you are—
trapped, heavy and visible
under the rain, only your vision
delicate as old leaves skimming
over the mounds of the seasons,
the limits of everything,
the few shaped bones of time.

        Mary Oliver, "At Blackwater Pond"[61]

Maps are essential gear for pilgrimages. It is not easy to use them without being led astray.

First, we need to recover our connections with flesh and soil. Then we can share stories about our journeys into those regions and raise puzzles about them. There comes a time when we must reflect and plan for the tasks facing us, at which point we can get help from maps.

Everyone learns at least in the first year of college that "the map is not the territory." A facile phrase, widely taken for granted. But it is not so easy determining which is which and how they are related. As you have read, I made some crucial errors in using Roman Catholic, Jesuit and Rolf maps. I assumed that there existed an already drawn map of that primal territory which I dreamed existed beyond the flatlands of the Sacramento Delta. I gave my life over to shopping for that map, angered and frustrated when successive candidates failed to lead me to that goal. Whenever I happened to stumble across a map that looked promising, I argued and cajoled everyone else to get on that road with me, feeling alienated from those who refused — always a very large number, of course.

The tendency to confuse ready-made abstract maps with the wild territories of personal life is a disease of the spiritual life inhibiting our efforts to make sense of things; at worst, twisting the passion of visionary experiences into pretentiousness. This tendency is not unique to the six body-spirit institutions and ecosystems that I have described. It surfaces in virtually every community that associates itself with a vision of life and has mapped out steps for locating it: religions, psychoanalytic and Somatics institutes, schools of psychological and social thought, Twelve Step programs. It even appears among scientists when they move beyond the limits of their data and quantitative methods to make pronouncements about the True and the Good.

Although it is tempting to jettison maps and set off across uncharted wilderness, that is not a viable solution for the major challenges that confront us. The Four Evangelists had to embellish the stories of Jesus to make sense of them for an ever wider audience of initiates, most of whom had no familiarity with the argot of Aramaic. Ignatius of Loyola had to unpack the meanings embedded in his visions on the Cardoner River for his young students at the Sorbonne, the first Jesuits. For Ida Rolf, a simple recording of her experiments working with friends and others could not have enabled her to design a school for hundreds of health practitioners; she had to create some kind of systematization. In the case of the graduate studies program which I direct, stories are not sufficient to help students shape their vision of their future professional work and prepare for such work, let alone gain a stamp of approval from state and national agencies. In addition to awakening a spirit of wonder and acquainting students with how actual innovators embody that spirit, we are faced with the challenge of how to enable students to develop the kind of intellectual clarity that will enable them to negotiate the rough waters of working with people on the edges of death and madness.

I AM A CHRONIC map-user. I had to learn how to make geographical maps as a civil engineering student in college. I have always used maps for hiking through the wilderness and finding my way through foreign countries. I regularly turn to maps of the body —both Western anatomical atlases and maps from other cultures—as a fundamental means for advancing my knowledge and practical skills.

If you know how to interpret them, maps can lead one into new experiences. USCGS maps contain clues about hidden canyons, hot springs and unexcavated archaeological ruins. Using them in that way, I have been able to find my way to remote mountain lakes where my wife and I can spend weekends in the middle of August, camping in isolation. Studying anatomical maps in that same spirit has led me into new methods for dealing with my back pain. For many years, I had guided my work by maps of muscles, bones and lungs. I had become increasingly familiar with the networks of muscles in my torso, the tiny interspinous ones and the long ones that run the length of the back. I began to understand how to relieve stress in them by a complex variety of stretching exercises. Pulmonary maps had given me the sense of how I might use breathing to relieve the knots in my torso. I sought out help from Somatics therapists like Rolfers and Feldenkrais practitioners who organized their work primarily on the basis of these maps. Their manipulations consisted largely of stretching taut muscle groups, or moving them in directions that would dissolve accumulated stress.

But many regions of the body remained opaque to me; for example, the interiors of the spinal column. Cross-sectional maps show the column filled with several layers of soft tissue and fluid. Some wildly imaginative anatomist named them the three mothers: the membranes of the *pia* (tender) and *arachnoid* (spider-like) *maters,* with their delicate laces immersed in spinal fluid, both surrounded by the *dura* (tough) *mater.* The spinal cord contains the complex structures of veins, arteries and nerves that exist in the brain from which it flows. As I became familiar with these maps, I wondered why my experience of my spinal column was so dry and brittle. It reflected none of the moisture or fleshiness these maps seemed to suggest.

I had learned from Ida Rolf that the creators of osteopathy, Andrew Still and William Sutherland, based their work on the theory that special kinds of manipulation could stimulate the flow of the cerebrospinous fluids, with dramatically effective results for healing many ills. I eventually went to a well-known osteopath whom I have been seeing monthly over a period of several years.

The result is that my spinal column now feels to me more like it looks on those anatomical maps. I now experience a liquidity and consequent ease in my back that I have never known. The pain still comes and goes, but it is not as debilitating or absorbing.

༄༅

The key to protecting oneself against the seductions of confusing maps and territories is to become familiar with how any map is constructed. That principle guided me in detailing how Ida Rolf's experiments led to her particular map of the ideal body. Recurrent problems with maps arise because their users are unfamiliar with how they are made, or they have forgotten that any map, physical or spiritual, is constructed from an infinite variety of sensual details with a great deal of physical effort, involving endless cycles of trial and error.

When I was a civil engineering student at Santa Clara University, I had to learn how to make maps. It is at least as much a sensual, physical process as it is rational, requiring rigorous training in sensory awareness to do it. Before using any instruments, one has to develop an overall sense of the land to be mapped, as well as a feeling for its peculiarities, how the contours are arranged, where they are broken by swales and outcroppings. Only then can one learn how to use to advantage the transit and tape to track the shape and dimension of each contour. The surveyor's job requires physical strength and flexibility. Typically, he or she has to climb steep slopes through dense manzanita and poison oak, often in intense summer heat when snows or rains are not making the territory impassable. Back in the office, there is the painstaking process of transferring the notebook record of those observations onto the velum itself and drawing the fine lines to connect the myriad dots.

To claim expertise, the mapmaker has to be more familiar with a particular region of the cosmos—a country, a nebula, a region of the biological world, the stages of meditation practice—than anyone else. Gaining such familiarity carries its own demands. The

mapmaker needs personal skills and the facility with any equipment or unique instruments necessary to explore a particular region.
Physical stamina has to be cultivated by those who would explore
remote terrains. The astronomer, anatomist or microbiologist must
learn how to use the elaborate technologies that yield the outlines
of those territories. The spiritual cartographer needs to be practiced in negotiating the wilds of altered states of consciousness.

To avoid being deceived by any map, one has to keep constantly
in mind that maps eliminate the infinite details irrelevant to the
mapmaker's specific purposes. A Chevron map of California is
appropriate for finding one's way among major cities on the inter-
state highways, but if you want to find a cul-de-sac on San Francisco's Telegraph Hill or in the back roads of the Topanga Canyon,
you had better get a local map. Or if you want to plot a backpack-
ing trip in the high Sierras, you will need a USCGS topographical
section map.

Until I went there in 1979, I thought that one-hundred miles on
a French map were equivalent to one-hundred California miles.
On that assumption, Elissa and I planned to cover most of France,
Great Britain, Ireland, Spain, Italy and parts of Scandinavia by
car within the three months we had for our trip. We abruptly skid-
ded to a crawl as we discovered that every mile was dense with
history, cuisine and hospitable people, to be relished for days, not
hours. Stopping in a Normandy village, with its Calvados, brie,
shellfish and patés was not like stopping for lunch at Denny's in
Vacaville.

Ignorance of the omitted details can be dangerous. In 1985, the
San Francisco Chamber of Commerce issued to tourists an imag-
inatively constructed map which pictured the highlights of the city
with only rough approximations of their geometrical positions.
For example, the Civic Center appeared to be an easy walk from the
long arm of Golden Gate Park called the Panhandle, which is
actually a distance of two hilly miles, much too far for older or
disabled visitors. And it routed visitors through the worst crime
section in the city, not portrayed on the map. Scores of tourists

ended up being assaulted and robbed every day. It's not that the map was bad; it gave a very good image of how one might plan a two- or three-day tour around the city. At the same time, without the additional aid of a precise grid and verbal descriptions about the neighborhood, it was dangerous.

The Germans and French are masters in this arena. The Baedeker and Michelin Guides give a combination of geometric plans of countries and cities with minute verbal descriptions of the terrain, historical monuments, views, lodgings and restaurants. The Michelin Green and Red Guides, with their stars, little houses and benches, rocking horses and dogs give the user a sense of the variety of choices that can be made in moving through a particular area. Qualities of food and its presentation, pleasantness of roads, expansiveness of a view, the range of art in a particular museum, the comparative value of visiting a given castle, and the tranquility of certain inns is described with as much specificity as you find in texts of Catholic moral theology.

Neuilly-sur-Seine 92200 Hauts-de-Seine 🏤 ⑤, 🔢 G. Paris – 64 450 h.

Voir Bois de Boulogne★★ : Jardin d'acclimatation★, Bagatelle★, Musée National des Arts et Traditions Populaires★★ — Palais des Congrès★ : grand auditorium★★, ◄★ de la tour Concorde-La Fayette.

Paris 8 – Argenteuil 12 – Nanterre 5,5 – Pontoise 37 – St-Germain 14 – Versailles 18.

🏨 **L'Hôtel International de Paris** Ⓜ, 58 bd V.-Hugo ℰ 47 58 11 00, Télex 610971, 🍴, Ambiance club, 🚗 – 🛗 🛎 📺 🕿 – 🅰 120 🆎 ⓞ Ε 🚾   M 18
R 220 bc – ⬜ 50 – **323 ch** 825/945, 3 appartements.

🏨 **Paris Neuilly** Ⓜ sans rest, 1 av. Madrid ℰ 47 47 14 67, Télex 613170 – 🛗 🛎 📺
🕿. 🆎 ⓞ Ε 🚾   N 16
⬜ 42 – **74 ch** 810/550, 6 appartements 700.

🏨 **Parc Neuilly** sans rest, 4 bd Parc ℰ 46 24 32 62, Télex 613689 – 🛗 📺 ⊖wc
🚻wc 🕿. 🚾   L 17
⬜ 20 – **71 ch** 220/390.

🏨 **Roule** sans rest, 37 bis av. du Roule ℰ 46 24 60 09 – 🛗 📺 ⊖wc 🚻wc 🕿. Ε 🚾
🅿   N 18
⬜ 22 – **35 ch** 200/320.

XXX ⚙ **Jacqueline Fénix**, 42 av. Ch.-de-Gaulle ℰ 46 24 42 61 – 🍽. 🆎 🚾   N 18
fermé août, 24 déc. au 3 janv., sam. et dim. – **R** (nombre de couverts limité – prévenir) carte 265 à 375
Spéc. Noix de St-Jacques en robe des champs (oct. à mars), Bar à la fleur de sel et vinaigrette au beurre noisette, Daube de lapereau au basilic.

Using these guides is a training in adult responsibility; they demand that you order your priorities at every turn. How much do you want to spend on a meal and room? Given that, would you like to eat a grand meal in a simple setting, or an ordinary meal in a more luxuriant setting? Would you like an elegant room in an old chateau in a quiet village in the hills or a simple room in an elegant hotel near the central plaza of a major city? Would you like to take a two-hour drive on the autoroute from Rome to Florence, or a six-hour drive on picturesque country roads, stopping at the three-starred Assisi and Fiesole?

By contrast, another elaborate series of French maps and texts, *Les sentiers des grandes randonnées*, "paths of the great trails," which give the user the possibility of taking walks throughout the whole of France, ranging from an hour to weeks, puts severe restrictions on the range of choices. By a combination of geometrical plans, detailed verbal descriptions and painted codes on fences and telephone poles, the walker is guided through what are judged to be "worthwhile" sights—medieval alleyways, meadows, small forest barriers—without ever having to look at a slum, factory or commercial center. One is even given directions to remote bus and train stops, with schedules. If you are spending a few days in Paris and have time for six hours in the country, *Les sentiers* can show you how you can take the nearest train for a forty-five-minute ride to the suburbs, walk for four hours through picturesque alleys, river banks and meadows, stopping for lunch at a local cafe, and mount a train in time to return to Paris for the evening.

But while the Michelin lays out its systems of judgments and codes so that its user is given a feeling for the enormous variety of choices that are available in any region of a tour, *Les sentiers*, like the Rolf Template, leaves no choice at all; it is so detailed that one cannot leave any particular route without peril. I have never been so lost as when I decided to explore an alley or pathway out of kilter with its prescribed directions. I would find myself in a desolate village with no way of finding out directions to the nearest bus or train.

SOMATICS TEACHERS BEGAN to use anatomical maps at the beginning of this century in a peculiar way that has led to a recovery of links between *body* and *spirit* which were severed at the outset of Western anatomical science four-hundred years earlier.

In older cultures, maps of the body are typically derived from, and associated with healing and spiritual practices. They are records of centuries of using meditation techniques and ritual movement to cultivate regions of the spinal column, the heart, lungs and areas of the brain, and to heal specific kinds of diseases associated with those different regions. Those classical maps embody the discovery that certain predictable states of consciousness, with characteristic images and feelings, are made accessible by long practice of dwelling within certain remote regions of experience. Acupuncture meridians, for example, are expressions of ordering the experiences had over centuries by such practices as qi gong, t'ai chi chu'an, and kung fu combined with experiments in healing. Vedic maps of the body are based on long-established records of experience derived from Hindu methods of meditation.

Modern anatomical cartography represents a radical break with experiential methods in its use of the technologies of dissection, x-rays, photomicroscopy and computer-enhanced imaging to uncover the previously uncharted contours of the objectified physical body. Like astronomical and geographical maps, modern anatomical maps, of themselves, tell nothing of people's experience of themselves, the earth or the heavens, except for what can be detected by sight or by instruments. It has only been in recent years that Somatics practitioners have begun to use biomedical maps as clues for experiential investigations. Used in that way, many of us, while looking for things like periosteum or embodied anger, have been surprised to find anger, joy, the remission of cancer and transcendence. But as you have seen in the case of Ida Rolf, there are often confusions about the truth-status of such maps. Not prepared by spiritual practices as people were in earlier cultures for those surprises, mistakes have been made: sometimes practitioners have not honored fleeting glimpses of the spaciousness of spirit, drawn by the needs of the business world to the more constricted demands of healing symptoms. Sometimes, in the excitement of inspiration, communities adopt a missionary zeal that turns a humble pilgrimage of discovery into a crusade for truth. The essence of being a pilgrim, the requirement to make the journey oneself, is lost.

BONNIE BAINBRIDGE COHEN is unique in using biomedically derived anatomical maps in the most detailed fashion to bridge seeming gaps between *body* and *spirit*. By the time I met her in 1986, Bonnie had devoted over twenty years to the exploration of the connections between direct experiences of the self and the entire range of anatomical maps. She had arrived at what I would call a phenomenological atlas of the body. The history of how she came to engage in that cartography holds clues for how to use maps without falling into their seductions. I am going to tell these details of Bonnie's map-making because they point up the depths of the problem which I am addressing in this book, that of becoming aware that any abstract view of reality is the expression of a lived perspective, situated in a particular place in time.

Bonnie grew up in the Ringling Brothers circus in Florida. Her mother, who had begun her career as a dancer on Broadway, performed balancing acts on the high platform and also Roman racing, where she stood astride two horses as they cantered around the ring. Bonnie's father had originally joined a small circus in California. When it was purchased by Ringling, he had taken a job with them as ticket-seller, and went on to become their publicity agent. As a young child, Bonnie remembers spending most of her time sitting in the middle of the three rings under the Big Top watching, watching. Few people ever spoke to her. Two who often did were Emmett Kelly, the famous sad clown, and the eldest of the Flying Wallendas, who paced up and down under the high wire waiting for one of his family to fall. She said that she identified more with him than with those on the wire above. When she reached school-age and the circus left Florida during the winter for its annual six-month tour, she was farmed out to a local family so she could remain in school. She grew up always feeling herself the outsider.

Her childhood way of dividing reality and fantasy was just the reverse of mine. Ordinary reality consisted of acrobats risking their lives on the highwire, the bearded lady and the snake lady. The structure of her everyday consciousness reflected the polymorphous quality of the three rings filled with horses, elephants, clowns, acrobats and fire-eaters, all performing simultaneously. Her fantasy land of Oz was simply "a house and a car." By contrast, I was surrounded by many systems that claimed to order the seeming chaos of experience: Roman Catholic theology, Western philosophy, my father's political and ethnic dogmas. These gave me the illusion that I had some grasp on the otherwise chaotic world of my night terrors and fears of diabolic possession. Bonnie had no contact with such explanatory schemes. To order life, she turned instead to the brilliant patterns inherent in the sophisticated physical skills of her mother, the Wallendas and Emmett Kelley. Her first language, she says, was movement. She used explorations of her own sense of movement as her primary guide through the various challenges of her life and uses it now as her primary means of communication.

Her childhood immersion in movement led her to look for a formal language that was close to her sensibility. English literature, history and social science were too remote from her three-ring imagination's habituation to rapidly adjusting muscles and tumbling bones. It was not until she reached high school courses in anatomy and physiology that she found a language close to her experience. She was so inspired by her first biology course that she appealed for permission to spend her entire senior year of high school doing a research project in anatomy based on dissecting a frog. She applied to Ohio State's School of Occupational Therapy, where her most important teachers were a married couple who had taught anatomy for forty years and were still vitally interested in their subject.

From 1962 to 1972, she worked with severely disabled adults and children. She was certified as a neuro-developmental therapist by the Bobaths in England, studied dance therapy with Marion Chace and neuro-muscular reeducation with André Bernard in New York. He was the first to make her explicitly aware of the possibilities of "embodying the maps of anatomy." She spent three years in Japan earning a living by developing a new school of occupational therapy for the Japanese Government. To do that required her to spend up to twelve hours a day reviewing anatomy so she could write it clearly enough for Japanese students who had the barest grasp of English. The tediousness of that task was the last of many straws that drove her to begin to depart from the healing practices based on the external orientation of biomedical maps to teach her own methods when she returned to the States in 1963.

At that point, she embarked on her life's work of the systematic investigation of the relations between experienced realities and biomedical maps. Experimenting on her own, she came to the discovery that each region of the lived body has its characteristic state of consciousness: images, feelings, sensations, intuitions about the world, perceptions of other people . . . in short, its own *mind.*

She goes about those experiments in this way. She will pose to herself the question: what is the *mind* of the bones? For as long as it takes—usually a year or more for each system, she says— she will spend hours a day working with movement and guided awareness to explore the regions mapped out by anatomical drawings of the bones of the body: the large and obvious bones of the legs and arms, as well as normally obscure bones, such as the metatarsals in the center of the foot, the tiny carpals in the hand and the cranial bones. Over the months, she familiarizes herself with the distinct qualities of this skeletal land, its associated images, memories, emotions, thoughts, tones of voice and qualties of movement rooted in that *mind.* After satisfying herself that she has gained enough information for now, she might shift her work to the *mind* of the nervous system, spending months focusing on the contours and weather patterns in that realm.

She has turned around the external reference of the original biomedical map towards the living experience of the self. Here is how she describes her method: "[I find these things] through the sensory feedback system. If you move your pelvis with your bones in your sensation, it registers one way; if you move your pelvis with your muscles in your sensation, it registers another way; if you move with your organs in mind then it registers differently." In the next sentence that follows that one, you can glimpse the ingenuity of her journeys: "Working with the glands, there was a body that I began to experience in myself and to see in others, that lay between the pituitary and the pineal on a diagonal line going up through the nose and through the back of the head. As we got in touch with that body, we found that the present, past and future all began to merge. Now, always and never."[62]

Each region requires specific keys for entry. In the case of the glands, for example, she uses this method: "[I open the glands] through breathing into that area. Through sounding into that area. Through a hissing breath. And then through moving. Once you've located a place it is easy to initiate movement from there. We watch for what mind comes out of that place; what actions come out of it; what are the efforts; what are the dynamics of that movement; what are the feelings and forms of that movement; what is the sound. All of that information comes out of that place. We experienced rebirthing and reincarnations while working with the glands. I had studied a discipline called "Katsugen Undo." It's a training of the involuntary nervous system developed by Noguchi Sensei in Japan. I was only briefly introduced to it but was very influenced by it. With the glands we went into automatic movement and watched what emerged."[63]

Over these years of work, she has reached the ability to discern with clarity the mind of one system of the body from another: "From the gland work, I went into the nervous system more carefully, contrasting the control of the nervous system and the brain with the control of the glands. Working with the brain as a major control system after working with the glands was moving from a very hot, emotional, volatile, chaotic system of energy and process to a cool system of organization, clarity and crystallization. There's a wildness to the glands and a sense of control in the nervous system."[64]

As that quote implies, her mapping is not confined to specific regions, but extends to relationships among regions: "If you are going to move one bone, another bone has to countersupport it. In the same way, if you are working with the nervous system, you balance it with the endocrine system and if you're in the endocrine, you support it with the nervous system."[65]

By exploring the layers of experience rooted in different regions of the body, she has woven an intricate system for touching other people and giving them movement instructions which will lead them into unfamiliar regions of experience. She can focus so intently on her bones as distinct from her muscles as distinct from her organs, that her touch and movement instructions can help others find those same areas. "If I'm working with any area of someone else's body, I will go into that area of my own body to see. In the process I become more open also. It becomes like two bells ringing on the same pitch. We can resonate each other."[66]

She has derived from these investigations a wide range of methods of touch and body movement direction, which she continues to apply successfully to the treatment of the most severe disorders ranging from brain-damage to asthma.

Her moving me with her hands and giving me directions for moving were the keys that enabled me to decipher the codes of her verbal language. She once worked with me lying on my back, while she sat behind me, hands cradling the occipital region of my head. She said, "Now I am in my bones moving your bones." I experienced unusually clear feelings of my cranial bones and the articulations of my skull and the vertebrae of my neck. I told her of my arid spinal sense. She continued, "I will go into my fluids...."

Now I am in my fluids." As she gently cradled my head and rocked it, I felt the gushing of fluids contained in my head and neck, followed by vibrant pulsings inside my spinal column. It felt like oil flowing deeply through my bones, so unfamiliar that my mind went blank for a moment, and I felt an ecstatic pleasure.

It is important to note that Bonnie uses maps with a radically different viewpoint from anatomists, who construct maps from the externally observed body, using dissection, x-rays, photomicroscopy and computer-enhanced imaging. That science is deliberately designed to exclude personal human experience so as to gain fragments of reliable knowledge purged of idiosyncratic biases. It provides maps of the body which are of the same order as topographical maps of the Rio Grande Basin, which do not pretend to tell anything of the ancient cultures there, nor of the Spanish invaders, nor of present day economic rapacity. Bonnie has found a method for systematically linking the information contained in the brilliant array of biomedical maps with the wealth of knowledge present in personal experience. While others have shown that contemporary maps of subatomic particles and galaxies are in accord with older spiritual cosmologies, she has done that task with biomedical maps.

She knows that her maps cannot capture the territory. In this passage, she accurately describes the immediacy of how I have experienced her working with myself and others. It is in no way distant, conceptual or dogmatic:

> ... in working with babies and people in general, I rarely work with the patterns directly; I'm working always with the space between the patterns. That's my strength. My weakness is I don't see objects. I'm the person who's doing all the work with all the body systems and getting movement down to one kind of concreteness. But I don't *see* that way. I work always with energy. I translate it into this physical structure, but I never work for myself from the physical structures. In my own vision, I see all the space but I see

poorly the structures in the space; I don't look at the movement, but the shadow of the movement.[67]

Often finding competing versions purportedly explaining the same realities, she knows the deceptiveness of any finally defined truth. For example, she tells of studying in England with Dr. and Mrs. Bobath while they worked with children with brain dysfunction:

> I saw that the new truths that I had were in conflict with theirs. I began to see that whenever I came to a truth, there was only a block in understanding. . . . I realized that I had to give up all the truths I had learned or discovered about the skeletal-muscular system in order to see what was actually happening.[68]

But like myself, Bonnie has had to struggle to extricate herself from the snares of the public language which she learned to speak as an adult. In my case, Graeco-Latin abstract words, and academic formalities have made it difficult for me to write about the fleshy territories where I have conducted my expeditions. In a similar way, the abstractions of medical language make Bonnie's radically experiential discoveries about how to find one's way into obscure wildernesses of the self sound distant and formal. The quotes I have cited above are hard to find in her extensive writings. I have had to listen carefully to her words, push her in personal conversations, and riffle through her texts to find those sentences that spell out the wild and ingenious ways that she has followed to arrive at her abstract formulations. In this more typical example of how she speaks of her discoveries, you can see how the language belies the radically experiential character of her work, the immediacy of her presence to other people, her wide-ranging imagination:

"The Dancer's Warm-up"

Fluid System

- Initiating and expressing movement through the fluid system, relates to the dynamics of flow and the interplay between stillness and action. The fluids are about transformation—multi-expressions of one flow. However, each fluid brings out different qualities of movement and mind state.
- The blood circulatory system functions in nurturing, embracing, gentleness and the flowing towards and away from ourselves and other selves. It establishes presentness and the flow between restful self and action.
  —Venous flow is very cyclic, wavelike movement, alternately rising and falling.
  —Arterial flow is an expression of the heart beat based upon precise pulse, alternating action and rest.
- The lymphatic system deals with defense, survival, the setting of limits and the crystalization of action; and in combination with the cerebrospinal fluid, sets up spatial tension.
- The cerebrospinal fluid relates to meditative rest and the central core of unbounded self ... [69]

It is relatively easy, at least for a non-believer, to grasp the derivation of Catholic dogma or the Rolf Template from spatiotemporal viewpoints. Bonnie's spare poetry of body parts, however, easily creates an illusion of being close to what seems to be the hard edge of objective bones, muscles, blood, lymph and thymus gland. What could be more real? What could be less metaphorical? Her identification of the experience of specific bodily regions with characteristic states of consciousness is even more deceptive than Ida Rolf's or Françoise Mézieres's imaginary ideals because it is easier for disciples to think they have captured reality without subjecting themselves to the long and arduous pilgrimage that Bonnie continues to negotiate with as much daring as her mother standing astride two racing stallions. When you grasp how she has transformed biomedical literalism into poetry, you can escape the materialistic dogmatism that identifies the maps with reality.

❧

UNDERSTANDING THE SPECIFIC ways that any particular map has been constructed—Bonnie's, Michelin, Taoist—illuminates the extent to which any particular ideal or set of values is applicable. The Chevron maps, the USCGS, the Michelin and Baedeker and *Les sentiers* have obvious value. Only a person who had never used them would argue that they could all be translated into a single comprehensive map or that the others could be eliminated by translating into a single one of them. There is, however, a sense in which each has a universal quality: anyone having the goals for which the map is designed—drive the fastest route from San Francisco to Los Angeles, spend three days visiting Madrid, take a six-hour walk near Saint Germain-en-Laye, backpack in the Sangre de Cristos—will find help in the relevant map whether or not that person is male or female, Jew or Christian, native American or Swedish, old or young.

I have described how exclusive reliance on a single map, for example the Rolf Template or the Christian map of the spiritual pilgrimage, can lead one into the difficulties faced by tourists armed only with that imaginary map of San Francisco. One needs something like the Michelin Red and Green Guides and the Baedekers, with their collections of maps, imaginary symbols and verbal descriptions. For example, if the upward verticality of the Rolf Template is situated within teachings about the wisdom of many dimensions of bodily direction, it becomes a vital component of teachings about the relation between *body* and *spirit.* Many practitioners who identify themselves as Rolfers are nurtured by that work, while at the same time maintaining affiliations with such radically different systems as Jungian analysis, *vipassana* meditation and Emilie Conrad Da'Oud's Continuum. Divorced from such alliances, the practice becomes a dogmatic verticalism. If Catholic sacramental theology's marriage of *body* and *spirit* is used to map the course of human life without the correctives of psychology, biological science and sociology, it can be used to support Roman authoritarianism. But used along with those other maps, it can lead a person to notice experiences that offset tendencies towards Cartesian dualism and crass materialism. In the hands of people like Teilhard de Chardin, Thomas Berry and the liberation theologians, the sacramental maps have become the underlying theory of an ecologically-oriented and politically-activist spirituality. Many Jesuits have pursued maps of spiritual practice created by Hindus, Sufis and Buddhists in addition to the "Exercises of Saint Ignatius." Many men and women derive nurture from the white-male Western body of knowledge exemplified in Plato, Chaucer, Shakespeare, Descartes, Marx and Freud, while recognizing that their fragments of wisdom cry out for ethnic and feminist additives.

Organizing one's life according to a particular set of maps—Jesuit, Sufi, biomedical, psychoanalytic—is like being with a group of trekkers moving along a particular route; other people hiking in the same region, some right next to us, walking side by side. We can sit together at the camp-fire poring over maps of the area, helping each other sort out the best ways to move ahead. If someone gets injured, we rush to help. But neither our maps nor our gear would fit groups of people maneuvering through different ecosystems.

In addition to local maps, some maps reflect the fact that all pilgrims share the same territory even if the paths are so distant that we will never encounter each other along the way. The valleys created by the Sacramento River, the Ganges, the Jordan, the Nile, the Rhine and the Yukon are worlds apart; many communities have mapped their watersheds and developed technologies for surviving in their climates. Despite their differences, we can now see on satellite weather maps how we are all buffeted by the same jet streams and ocean currents and protected by a single diaphanous veil of ozone.

Lines and images are not enough. A USCGS map cannot, of its nature, tell its reader to take care of the environment; that will require a list of things either added to the map or put out on a Forest Service brochure: "Carry out your garbage," "Bury your fecal wastes," "Don't aggravate the bears by coming between mother and cub;" "Don't dispose of crank-case oil in the creek." The Cohen map of the bone marrow cannot give an account of how to journey into that fiery realm of energy. It needs verbal accounts, specific stories about how the novice might embark upon that complex journey and what gear might be needed.

The great spiritual texts—the Bible, *Koran, Upanishads, Tao Te Ching, I Ching,* the collections of native American and African stories—do not present clearly drawn maps like *Les sentiers,* the Rolf Template, the Freudian psychosexual stages or the prescriptions of Saint Ignatius's "Rules of Modesty." They contain aphorisms, paradoxical teachings and stories. Like the Michelin Guides, they open up a universe of infinite possibilities of choice. It is only at the second or third levels of interpretation of the primal spiritual texts by zealous disciples that you can find maps drawn with the illusory clarity of dogmatism.

Refugees from diverse cultures, we do not share a single set of normative stories, nor does any atlas satisfy the needs of everyone. But we can share stories of our not uncommon journeys, or, when the journey has been forgotten or suppressed, stories of what it is like to recover from a journey and settle into an unfamiliar place where one does not yet, if ever, feel at home.

The spirit lurks somewhere in the interstices between maps and territories ... when directions fail, leaving room for being surprised by love, wisdom and a sense of humor.

WHEN I VISIT strange places, instead of making those kinds of contacts with strangers that often happen in the course of asking directions, I bury myself in maps. And since maps gloss over the back alley-ways, or leave out indications that one street is separated from another by a two-hundred-foot cliff, I often get needlessly lost. Instead of sniffing out my way through such places in easy contact with the inhabitants, I try to follow abstract lines on paper. In past chapters, I have described some of the deliberate efforts I have had to make to turn away from a natural absorption in maps towards more primal territories, attempting to find more immediate relationships to people and locales. Maps cannot tell where a turn down an alley might lead to an encounter with another person that might change our lives.

Within the field of Somatics, the maps often have the seductive effect of drawing the practitioner away from a sense of immediate contact with the person into abstract ideas about the work.

THE DEEPER I plunged into those murky realms between familiar terrain and already drawn maps, the more I encountered a strange paradox. As I become more aware of the particularity of my immersion in the Pacific world, jostling along with my nearly inflexible spinal column, I feel more connected with other people, as well as animals, trees and earth. When I feel that one map accounts for reality, I am alienated from those who do not follow that map—an inevitably large population no matter what map one chooses. Insofar as I feel that "reality" can be adequately described only by an unimaginably large variety of maps, texts, images and stories, I am impelled to become engaged with the cartographers who have threaded their way through lands unknown to me.

Strangely enough, the breakdown of the idealism that had driven my life forward for fifty years was accompanied by a sense of relief. The illusion that it was possible for me—and therefore my moral responsibility—to give voice to a universal viewpoint in comparison to which all other viewpoints were thought to be partial or erroneous, was a heavy burden. No wonder I had a stiff spine. Now I could relax into particularity. Strangely enough, that particularity was not solipsistic. The more I became aware of the unique qualities of my perspective, rooted in the paths I stumbled along to reach a particular vantage point, using my peculiar bones and hormonal arrangements, the more I became able to listen in silence to the stories other people tell, without trying to translate them into versions of mine.

※

Somatics has helped many of us who had lost our way tracking already drawn maps. In the absence of a literal ancestral home and village, the strategies of the various Somatics practices create a new sense of belonging. Rolfing can awaken a sense of belonging within the earth's field of gravity. Sensory Awareness makes us alive to our situation within air currents, smells, trees and street noise. Feldenkrais creates a necessary sense of ease within the inevitable flux of people and events. Continuum and Body-Mind Centering make us at home with the pulsing of our cells, blood and lymph. All of those methods, and others like them, are capable of restoring our recognition of the many senses of connection that bind us with our neighbors.

The Alexander Technique provides equipment for meeting an ever-recurrent challenge along the way: that of preserving a rich sense of the present moment along with a vision of the future. When F. M. Alexander finally unraveled the dynamics that led to his habit of constricting his throat each time he set foot on the stage to perform, he came to a distinction between "end-gaining" and "means-whereby." "End-gaining" is the obsession with the goal to be obtained (in his case, "pleasing the audience") to such a degree that one does not notice the infinity of self-defeating means whereby one is moving between here and there ("tightening the back of the neck," "arching the back," etc.). His distinction illuminates the twofold task of the pilgrim. It is indeed necessary to maintain the passion for one's ideals, the goals that give meaning to the dreariness of getting up each morning. But one of the crucial errors made by pilgrims is to put their primary attention on the final destination, failing to recognize that spiritual reality exists everywhere in the "means-whereby" along the way: in stopping to help the sick man lying beside the road, accepting an invitation to listen to the stories told by an old woman living in a hut in the forest, taking time to pay careful attention to nightly dreams. Here is where divinity unfolds, along the way, not simply at the sacred shrine towards which one is traveling.

NOTES

1. Rumi, *Unseen Rain: Quatrains of Rumi,* trans. John Moyne and Coleman Barks (Putney, VT: Threshold Books, 1986), 1.

Chapter One: Points of View

2. The term was originally coined by the late Thomas Hanna, the founder and editor of the journal *Somatics.* He defines it in this way: "Somatics is the field which studies the *soma:* namely, the body as perceived from within by first-person perception. When a human being is observed from the outside—i.e., from a third-person viewpoint—the phenomenon of a human *body* is perceived. But when this same human being is observed from the first-person viewpoint of his own proprioceptive senses, a categorically different phenomenon is perceived: the human *soma.*" *Somatics* 5, no. 4 (Spring/Summer 1986), 4.

3. For fragments of this forgotten lineage, I am indebted to two lovely books written by its direct heirs: Carola H. Speads, *Ways to Better Breathing* (Great Neck, NY: Felix Morrow, 1986), xxi ff.; and Dr. Lilly Ehrenfried, *De l'éducation du corps à l'équilibre de l'esprit* (Paris: *Éditions Montaigne,* 1956), 133–139. The task of uncovering the history of Somatics is similar to that confronting feminist historians; we depend on oral history, fragments mentioned by the way in exercise books or in histories of dance, a teacher mentioned in passing.

4. The American folk healing arts of osteopathy and chiropractic, with their elaborate hands-on strategies, are intimately related to this field. I have not given them a major place in this story simply because their decision to accede to the demands of the American Medical Association forced them into rigidly conventional educational systems with little emphasis on the manipulative medicine which constituted their original genius.

5. As this book is going to print, a team of us is embarking on the first major empirical study of Somatics, an investigation of the efficacy of various Somatics methods for alleviating chronic low-back pain.

Section I: Body-Spirit Institutions

6. Mary Oliver, *House of Light* (Boston: Beacon, 1990), 1.

Chapter Two: Incarnation

7. There has been a spate of academic literature in the past few years describing the centrality of the body in the earliest understandings of Christianity. Contrary to anachronistic readings of the tradition in light of modern repressive notions of the body and sex, these writers argue that the early notions were in fact revolutionary. Cf., for example, Peter Brown, *The Body and Society: Men, Women, and Sexual Renunciation in Early Christianity* (New York: Columbia, L988); and Margaret Miles, *Carnal Knowing: Female Nakedness and Religious Meaning in the Christian West* (Boston: Beacon, 1989).

8. *San Francisco Chronicle* (UPI), 30 March 1985, 5.

9. "The Penitential of Cummean," II, 6, from *The Irish Penitentials*, ed. Ludwig Bieler (Oxford: Oxford University Press, 1963).

10. "A Book of David," #8 and #9, from *Medieval Handbooks of Penance*, ed. John T. McNeill and Helena Gamer (New York: Octagon Books, 1965).

11. Rev. Heribert Jone, *Moral Theology*, "Englished and Adapted to the Laws and Customs of the United States of America" by Rev. Urban Adelman (Westminster, MD: Newman Press, 1963), 228.

12. Ibid., 228.

13. Quoted by Elizabeth H. and Joseph H. Pleck in *The American Man* (Englewood Cliffs: Prentice-Hall, L980), 225.

14. Ibid., 236–7.

Chapter Three: Esoteric Impulses

15. *The Spiritual Exercises of St. Ignatius,* "Rules for Thinking with the Church," #365.

16. "The Constitutions of the Society of Jesus," Part VI, ch. 1, #547.

17. Gregory Bateson, "Toward a Theory of Schizophrenia" in *Steps to an Ecology of Mind* (New York: Random House/Ballantine, L978), 208.

18. *The Spiritual Exercises of St. Ignatius*, #23.

19. Leo Steinberg, *The Sexuality of Christ in Renaissance Art and in Modern Oblivion* (New York: Pantheon, 1983).

20. There is a similarity between the Ignatian injunction against touch and the Freudian. Dogmatic psychoanalysts reject Somatic psychotherapy on the assumption that the use of touch in the therapeutic relationship is so powerful that it makes it impossible for the patient and the analyst to resolve the transference provoked by it.

21. Michel Foucault, "The Battle for Chastity," from *Western Sexuality: Prac-*

tice and Precept in Past and Present Times, ed. Phillipe Aries and Andre Bejin (New York: Blackwell, 1986), 24.

Chapter Four: Desires, Primal and Acquired

22. Don Hanlon Johnson, "Desire as the Basis of Thomistic Ethics," *The Modern Schoolman* (Spring 1963), 22–35; "Lonergan and the Redoing of Ethics," *Continuum* 5, no. 2 (Summer 1967), 211–220. These two articles, particularly the first, give all the relevant references to Aristotle and Aquinas.

Chapter Six: Vertical Enlightenment: Ida Rolf

23. John E. Upledger, *Craniosacral Therapy, Somatoemotional Release* (Berkeley: North Atlantic Books, 1993); John E. Upledger and Jon D. Vredevoogd, *Craniosacral Therapy* (Seattle: Eastland Press, 1983).
24. Rosemary Feitis, "An interview with Rosemary Feitis," *The Bulletin of Structural Integration* (December 1976), 2.
25. *Ida Rolf Talks About Rolfing and Physical Reality,* ed. Rosemary Feitis (New York: Harper and Row, 1978), 10. Much of the material in this chapter comes from Rosemary's illuminating interviews with Ida. I recommend this book, rather than Ida's own, *Rolfing: The Integration of Human Structures* (New York: Harper, 1979) for anyone interested in Rolfing, because it gives the reader a feel for Ida's ingenious ways of thinking and imagining, more so than her own more formal account.
26. Shinryu Suzuki Roshi, *Zen Mind, Beginner's Mind* (New York, Tokyo: John Weatherhill, 1980), 25.
27. Yuasa Yasuo, *The Body* (trans. Nagatomo Shigenori, T. P. Kasulis, Albany: State University of New York, 1987), 100.
28. Ida Rolf, *Rolfing: The Integration of Human Structures* (New York: Harper and Row, 1978).
29. "Dr. Rolf Says . . . ," from *Rolf Lines* (December 1977), 3.

Section II
Chapter Seven: Between Cultures

30. *Ida Rolf Talks About,* 108.
31. Fritjof Schuon, *From the Divine to the Human* (Bloomington, IN: World Wisdom Books, 1982), quoted without page reference in *Parabola* 10, no. 3 (August 1985), 38.
32. Timothy White, "An Interview with Johnny Moses," *Shaman's Drum,* no. 23 (Spring 1991), 38. I wrote an account of the breakdown in my

dogmatic verticalism: "The Body: The Cathedral and the Kiva," in *In Search of a Therapy*, ed. Dennis Jaffe (New York: Harper and Row, 1977).

33. Rene Cailliet, M.D., *Neck and Arm Pain* (Philadelphia: F. A. Davis Company, 1964), 9.

34. Marcel Mauss, "The Techniques of the Body," trans. B. Brewer, *Economy and Society* 2 (1973), 70–88. See also the subsequent work of Mary Douglas, *Natural Symbols* (New York: Pantheon, 1982), and Pierre Bourdieu, *Distinction: A Critique of the Judgement of Taste*, trans. Richard Nice (Cambridge, MA: Harvard, 1984).

35. Carolyn Shaffer, "An Interview with Emilie Conrad Da'Oud," *The Yoga Journal*, no. 77, (Nov./Dec. 1987), 52.

36. Ibid., 52.

37. Irene Lober, *Auf eigenen Füssen gehen: Somato-psychologische Erfahrungen einer ehemals Querschnittsgelähmten* (Lohrbach: Der Grüne Zweig, 1989).

Chapter Eight: Scarred Bodies/Broken Hearts

38. Thérèse Bertherat, *The Body Has Its Reasons*, trans. Carol Bernstein (New York: Avon, 1979), 92.

39. Dr. Lilly Ehrenfried, see note 3.

40. Don Hanlon Johnson, *Body* (Berkeley, CA: North Atlantic Books, 1992).

41. Don Hanlon Johnson, "Somatic Platonism," *Somatics* 3, no. 1 (Autumn 1980), 4–7; followed up by "Principles versus Techniques: Towards the Unity of the Somatics Field," *Somatics* 6, no. 1 (Autumn/Winter 1986–87), 4–8.

Chapter Nine: Male Vociferousness

42. Bonnie Bainbridge Cohen, *Sensing, Feeling and Action: The Experiential Anatomy of Body-Mind Centering* (Northampton, MA: Contact Editions, 1993), 96 (italics mine).

Section III
Chapter Ten: The Spirit of Wonder

43. Moshe Feldenkrais, *Body Awareness As Healing Therapy: The Case of Nora* (Berkeley, CA: North Atlantic Books, 1993), 7.

44. In addition to the texts cited in the notes for this chapter, I have derived the material from a 1992 private video (filmed by Judyth Weaver) of Charlotte talking about her life with a group of students, and from several personal conversations extending over a period from 1987 to 1993.

45. The development of the Delsarte System is described in Ted Shawn's

Every Little Movement (New York: M. Wittmark, 1954), which also has a bibliography of the work.

46. Leo Kofler, *The Art of Breathing* (New York: Edgar S. Werner, 1889); German edition (Cassel, Germany: Baerenreiter Verlag, 23rd edition, 1966).

47. Ilana Rubenfeld, "Interview with Ilana Rubenfeld," *Somatics* 1, no. 2 (Spring 1977), 14, revised by Charlotte in her reading of this manuscript.

48. Ibid., 14.

49. Ibid., 14.

50. Ibid., 15.

51. Charles Brooks, *Sensory Awareness* (Great Neck, NY: Felix Morrow, 1986), 231. In the last months of World War II, the Nazis bombed Gindler's studio because of her activities in hiding Jewish students. Of her many papers, only one has survived, "Gymnastic for Everyone," trans. The Charlotte Selver Foundation, *Somatics* 6, no. 1 (Autumn/Winter 1986–87), 35–39.

52. John Schick, "Interview with Charlotte," *The Sensory Awareness Foundation Newsletter* (Winter 1987), 2. (This newsletter is published at 273 Star Route, Muir Beach, CA 94965.)

53. The self-styled "barefoot phenomenologist" Elizabeth Behnke has drawn a brilliant comparison of the two bodies of knowledge: "Sensory Awareness and Phenomenology: A Convergence of Traditions," *The Newsletter of the Study Project in Phenomenology of the Body* 2, no. 1 (Spring 1989), 27–42. (Available from P. O. Box O–2, Felton, CA 95018.)

54. *Sensory Awareness*, 7.

55. "Interview with Charlotte," 3.

56. Ibid., 2.

57. Ibid., 2.

58. "Interview with Ilana Rubenfeld," 17.

Chapter Eleven: Life Stories and Abstract Theories

59. Gregory Bateson, *Mind and Nature: A Necessary Unity* (New York: Bantam, 1980), 14.

60. Caroline Walker Bynum, *Fragmentation and Redemption: Essays on Gender and the Human Body in Medieval Religion* (New York: Zone Books, 1991), 24–5.

Chapter Twelve: Body-Spirit Maps

61. Mary Oliver, *Twelve Moons* (Boston: Little, Brown, 1979), 49.

62. Nancy Stark Smith, "Interview with Bonnie Bainbridge Cohen," *Contact Quarterly*, no. 1 (1981), 7.
63. Ibid, 7.
64. Ibid, 7.
65. Ibid, 8.
66. Ibid., 5.
67. Bonnie Bainbridge Cohen, "Perceiving in Action," *Contact Quarterly* (Spring/Summer 1984), 39.
68. "Interview with Bonnie Bainbridge Cohen," 6.
69. Bonnie Bainbridge Cohen, "The Dancer's Warm-up," *Contact Quarterly* (Fall 1988), 29.